GAUTAMA BUDDHA'S SUCCESSOR

GAUTAMA BUDDHA'S SUCCESSOR

A FORCE FOR GOOD IN OUR TIME

ROBERT POWELL
ESTELLE ISAACSON

Lindisfarne Books

2014

2013
LINDISFARNE BOOKS
AN IMPRINT OF STEINERBOOKS/ANTHROPOSOPHIC PRESS, INC.
610 Main St., Great Barrington, MA 01230
www.steinerbooks.org

Cover image: Statue depicting Maitreya,
Thikse Monastery, Ladakh, India
Design by William Jens Jensen

LIBRARY OF CONGRESS CONTROL NUMBER: 2013953818

ISBN: 978-1-58420-161-8 (paperback)
ISBN: 978-1-58420-162-5 (eBook)

Contents

Acknowledgments

The authors of this book express their heartfelt gratitude to Claudia McLaren Lainson for her foreword and her dedication in continuing research into the spiritual mysteries of our time, and with heartfelt thanks to Richard Bloedon for shepherding this book right from the beginning and for his skilled editorial assistance.

An immense debt of gratitude is owed to Rudolf Steiner (1861–1925) and Valentin Tomberg (1900–1973) for pioneering new knowledge in the twentieth century concerning the great spiritual teacher—or bodhisattva, to use the Sanskrit term—who will become the Maitreya Buddha by the middle of the fifth millennium.

We would also like to thank publisher Gene Gollogly of SteinerBooks for taking on the manuscript and enabling this book to become available, and William Jens Jensen for his meticulous work in making it possible for this book to appear in print.

There are many others who have helped in one way or another to whom our gratitude and appreciation are extended, without naming everyone explicitly.

Robert Powell and Estelle Isaacson
September 10, 2013—Sun at 22½° Leo:
Cosmic Festival of the Assumption of the Virgin Mary

GAUTAMA BUDDHA'S SUCCESSOR—
RUDOLF STEINER'S PROPHECY:

"The Bodhisattva who took the place of Gautama when he became Buddha will come in the form of the Maitreya Buddha.... He will be the greatest of the proclaimers of the Christ Impulse."

—RUDOLF STEINER,
"The Impulse of Christ and His Great Proclaimers,"
Rome, April 13, 1910

Foreword

Claudia McLaren Lainson

The year 2014 has a special significance that is addressed in this book by Robert Powell and Estelle Isaacson. Dr. Robert Powell is a spiritual researcher who in this short work—and in many other books—brings the results of his own research investigations. Estelle Isaacson is a seer gifted with a remarkable ability to perceive new streams of revelation. Both have been blessed in an extraordinary way by virtue of accessing the realm wherein Christ is presently found in an ethereal form. In this realm of life forces, or the etheric world that surrounds and envelopes the physical world, what lies beyond the normal threshold of consciousness is starting to weave into the spiritual perceptions of an increasing number of human beings. However, inner effort is needed for this to take place, because in our modern Western culture we are constantly bombarded by forces that are not conducive to spiritual awakening and that, as a priority on the spiritual path, have to be dealt with and overcome. These forces are, to a certain extent, caused by the effects of materialistic science and technology that have escalated at an unprecedented rate since the latter part of the twentieth century. A first step in the spiritual awakening to Christ's Second Coming, an awakening that opens one to knowledge and experience of Christ's living presence in the etheric world, the biosphere, entails encountering—or, rather, countering—those forces.[1]

---

1 See, for example, Powell, *Cultivating Inner Radiance and the Body of Immortality*, and Isaacson, *Through the Eyes of Mary Magdalene.*

The remarkably gifted Austrian philosopher and spiritual researcher Rudolf Steiner (1861–1925), who was recognized by many in Europe as a universal genius during the first quarter of the twentieth century, foretold that, from about 1933 onward, people would increasingly come into the presence of Christ in a new way—in an ethereal form appearing in the etheric world, the biosphere of life forces that permeates the whole of humankind and nature. The numerous experiences that have been reported by many people since then confirm the intrinsic authenticity of Steiner's words.[2] On the other hand, he also warned about the inevitable coming of an "embodiment of evil" as a force to counter the new presence of Christ's coming "in the clouds," which is the expression used in the Apocalypse of St. John: "Behold, he is coming in the clouds, and every eye will see him" (Rev. 1:7). Note that clouds, as the bearer of life-giving water for nature, offer an appropriate image for us to think of the Second Coming—the coming of Christ in the realm of life forces.

On November 1, 1919, Steiner pointed in a very concrete way to an embodiment, an actual incarnation, of an evil being to indwell a specific human being, and indicated that this incarnation would take place shortly after the beginning of the twenty-first century.[3] These two juxtaposed truths live side by side, for it is in relation to Christ's Second Coming that Ahriman has now chosen to incarnate into a human being liv-

---

2   Powell, *The Christ Mystery: Reflections on the Second Coming.*

3   Steiner, *The Incarnation of Ahriman: The Embodiment of Evil.*
This evil being was identified by Rudolf Steiner as the "evil twin" referred to in Zoroastrianism by the name Ahriman—the evil brother of the "good twin" known in the Zoroastrian religion as Ahura Mazda, meaning "Aura of the Sun." Without going into details as to why Steiner chose to refer to the "Prince of Darkness" by this name, it is evident that the opponent of Ahura Mazda—Ahriman of the Zoroastrian tradition—is the same as Seth, the opponent of Osiris in the Egyptian tradition, in turn identical with Satan in the Judeo-Christian tradition, whose embodiment in human form as the Antichrist is foretold in Revelations 13—the Antichrist ("the embodiment of evil") being referred to there as "the beast."

ing on the Earth. As is described in the following pages of this book, he is doing this in order to execute his plan of opposition to the Etheric Christ. (Let us note that "Ahriman"—an ancient Persian designation—is the name chosen by Rudolf Steiner to designate the evil being here under consideration). Ahriman's goals in taking on embodiment in human form are multiple and multi-layered. Certainly one of these goals is to thwart recognition of Christ's Second Coming; and to accomplish this necessitates blocking or even doing away with—or, at the very least, marginalizing—the messengers of Christ's coming "in the clouds," in the etheric realm.

In the first chapter of this publication and in the appendices, Robert Powell offers a far-reaching study. The fruits of his investigations uncover various profound truths that are not, however, for the faint of heart. His words, born of experience gained over many decades of intensive research, are intended first and foremost to reveal the actual circumstances prevailing in the world at the present time. The high degree of precision he applies in presenting his findings is noteworthy, as is his uncompromising stance. He stands courageously as a spiritual messenger in our time, well aware of the gravity of the facts revealed through his research.

Powell makes the critical point that the year 2014 denotes the beginning of a new six-hundred-year cultural wave in history and that there is also an ancient prophecy that can be interpreted as pointing to the onset of the twenty-first-century incarnation of the Maitreya Bodhisattva in this very year, 2014. Crucial to grasping this extraordinary historical convergence is a proper understanding of what a bodhisattva is and, in particular, of the bodhisattva who will become the future Maitreya Buddha awaited by Buddhists. Intrinsic to this understanding, as described in chapter 1, is that the bodhisattva who will become the Maitreya Buddha incarnates in almost every century and will become the Maitreya Buddha shortly before the year 4500. Moreover, 2014 is related to the incarnation in the twenty-first century of the bodhisattva who will become the Maitreya Buddha in some 2,500 years.

As pointed out in this book, the Maitreya Buddha, "the bearer of the good," is identical with the Kalki Avatar awaited in the Hindu tradition—Kalki being "the annihilator of ignorance." It is, therefore, a matter of the possible coming in our time of one of the great spiritual teachers of humanity—Maitreya-Kalki—a teacher who, as detailed in this book, evidently works in collaboration with the highest spiritual guidance spanning the width of the twentieth century and continues now in the twenty-first century. Alongside this prophecy is strong evidence showing that now is the prophesied time of the embodiment of evil that Steiner spoke of as the "incarnation of Ahriman."[4] This embodiment stands in stark contrast to the prophesied coming of the great spiritual teacher who is the "bearer of the good" (the literal translation of *Maitreya*).

For some readers, opening this book will be a first encounter with the mysteries of the bodhisattva destined to become the next buddha, the Maitreya Buddha. Here it has to be emphasized that the mission of the bodhisattva who will become the Maitreya Buddha stands completely in the service of Christ in his Second Coming in the etheric realm. With this work, it is clear that the intention of both Powell and Isaacson, who are clearly servants of this bodhisattva, and who are both aligned with this bodhisattva's mission of serving Christ in the etheric realm, is to help prepare readers for the emergence of this great teacher—one whose time has evidently come. If one assimilates the content of this book in an open-minded way, deepening into the images invoked herein, a breathtaking panorama is revealed. Just as Powell does not shy away from stating the hard facts about the true nature of the present time, so Isaacson does not turn her back on the gift of

---

4   Powell and Dann, *Christ and the Maya Calendar: 2012 and the Coming of the Antichrist*, and Powell, *Prophecy-Phenomena-Hope: The Real Meaning of the year 2012*.

seership that her destiny calls her to bear. The visions she shares in these pages penetrate the majestic spiritual heights and depths wherein the great teacher is found who is the focus of this book. In so doing, her words open us to the profound teachings currently emanating from the Bodhisattva Maitreya, who is the same individuality awaited in Hindu tradition as the future Kalki Avatar.

In appendix 1, Powell cites Steiner's references to the ten avatars of Hindu spiritual tradition. The last three of the ten avatars—Krishna, Gautama,[5] and Kalki—have missions that reveal the unfolding of the spiritual plan of evolution descending through various levels. Using a language that describes the subtle (non-physical) aspects of the human being, we can follow the progression of this evolutionary descent from the "I" to the astral body and to the etheric body. *"I"* refers here to the human self; the astral body relates to the soul; and the etheric body signifies the body of life forces that interpenetrate and maintain the physical body until the moment of death, when the etheric body separates from the physical body, leaving it behind as a corpse. Let us look at these three levels more closely in terms of the descending stream exemplified here by the three avatars: Krishna, Gautama Buddha, and Kalki.

The level of the "I": In his book *Christ and the Maya Calendar* (coauthored with Kevin Dann), Powell builds on Steiner's indications regarding Krishna.[6] In the case of Krishna, it is a matter of the "I" of a lofty and pure human being who had not undergone the Fall, who had not previously incarnated on the Earth, and who spoke to Arjuna the charioteer, revealing the content of the Bhagavad Gita. The Bhagavad Gita is essentially the narrative of the non-physical manifestation of the Krishna soul, who revealed himself to Arjuna as the Lord of all existence; non-physically, signifying that it was an "overlighting" of Arjuna by Krishna, who

---

5   See note by Robert Powell on page 120–121.

6   Powell and Dann, *Christ and the Maya Calendar*, p. 29.

was not physically incarnated. Rudolf Steiner discovered through spiritual research that Krishna did incarnate later in a single and unique incarnation as Jesus of Nazareth, whose birth is described in the Gospel of St. Luke. Steiner indicated, moreover, that Jesus of Nazareth was the one into whom Christ incarnated at the time of the baptism in the River Jordan.[7]

The soul level of the astral body, also known as the soul body: It was Gautama Buddha's transfigured astral body that brought him to enlightenment.[8] That incarnation was the last one of Gautama, who nevertheless continues to participate in humanity's unfolding spiritual evolution. For example, as Steiner indicates:

> The "Gloria" heard by the shepherds in the fields proclaimed from the spiritual world that the forces of Buddha were streaming into the astral body of the Jesus child described in St. Luke's Gospel. The words of the "Gloria" came from Buddha, who was working in the astral body of the Jesus child. This wonderful message of peace and love is an integral part of Buddha's contribution to Christianity.[9]

The life level of the etheric, or life, body: As revealed in the following pages, the power inherent in the words sounding forth from the Kalki–Maitreya individuality is permeated by Christ's body of life forces. According to Steiner, the bodhisattva who will become the Maitreya Buddha will develop the moral power of the word to an extraordinary degree (see appendix 1).

The Maitreya, as we are informed in chapter 1, will incarnate around the year 4443, at the end of the Age of Aquarius and

---

7   Ibid.

8   Steiner, *The Gospel of St. John*, lecture 12: "The astral body has to be cleansed, purified, ennobled, and subjected to catharsis; then a person may expect that the external spirit will stream into him for his illumination"—as was the case at the enlightenment of Gautama Buddha.

9   Steiner, *Esoteric Christianity and the Mission of Christian Rosenkreutz*, lecture 7.

leading into the Age of Capricorn, which starts in 4535.[10] Against this background, the enlightenment—or the ascent from bodhisattva to the Maitreya Buddha—will probably occur shortly before the year 4500, and the departure of the Maitreya Buddha from the earthly realm may occur shortly before or coincide with the start of the Age of Capricorn in 4535. Though these dates may seem too far in the future to concern us, in reality what is seeded now will flower later. This applies to the cultural development of humanity as a whole, as well as to the individual development of each of us. What we seed today will determine the influences we will encounter as we return to Earth in future incarnations. Becoming aware of contemporary spiritual reality thus prepares us to follow and subsequently take up the remarkable guidance of the great teachers through the coming ages of time. In this way we learn to understand the language that develops through spiritual evolution—for example, as it passes from one bodhisattva individuality to the next.

The soul can be seen as a garden that needs to be tended, and without the deep and profound spiritual nourishment offered by the great teachers, the bodhisattvas, the garden of the soul might remain fallow, unseeded, in relation to what should come as the future "harvest of the soul." To miss what the bodhisattvas are bringing—indeed, to miss what any of these great teachers brings to humanity—can unwittingly create a spiritual deficit for oneself and for our fellow human beings. This is especially true if it happens to be one's responsibility to communicate to others the significance of a particular teacher, including the content of that individuality's teaching.

As Robert Powell illumines the significance of the six-hundred-year rhythm of the cultural waves spoken of by Steiner, he guides us to be wakeful and alert as now a new cultural wave begins in 2014. In this connection he also depicts the ancient prophecy

---

10   Powell, *Hermetic Astrology*, vol. 1, p. 63.

relating to the possible reincarnation of the Maitreya–Kalki individuality in our time, to inaugurate the change this new cultural wave portends. He indicates the likelihood that there will be collaboration between the great spiritual streams inaugurated upon the Earth by Buddha and Christ. The confluence of these streams has the potential of ushering in a new age of a Christ-permeated Buddhism—that is, a renewed and enlivened Buddhism that receives the inspiration of Christ now flowing in as a result of his presence in the etheric world—this being the event known in Christian tradition as the "Second Coming." This new Christ-permeated Buddhism is intended to serve humanity's spiritual evolution and further the unfolding of the evolution of the Earth.

In Buddhist tradition, we are told that when Gautama Buddha indicated one of his disciples, the Bodhisattva Kashyapa, as his successor, he "raised a lotus blossom and blinked his eyes."[11] Likewise will the teachings of Kashyapa–Maitreya in the process of becoming the next Buddha raise the lotus blossom of the word so that our eye of spirit (the third eye) may quicken. In this quickening, the lotus flower of wisdom will be prepared—through the anticipated power of the word—to perceive the fact of his presence.[12] Through the "treasury of the eye of truth," we may come to understand this teacher's words. This, of course, will depend on each person's level of moral-spiritual development. The measure of moral development will provide a benchmark against the background of which a separation will emerge between those who have ears to hear and eyes to see, and those who—for whatever reason—cannot hear or see sufficiently to absorb the new teachings.

---

11   See chapter 1 of this book.

12   This statement presupposes that the ancient prophecy of the coming of the Kalki individuality is indeed fulfilled at this time beginning in 2014—always remembering that it is a matter of a prophecy, not a scientific fact, and therefore it remains to be seen whether this prophecy will actually be fulfilled. In addition, the possibility should be borne in mind that the prophecy could perhaps be fulfilled without this individuality necessarily appearing as a publicly recognizable figure.

Just as Gautama Buddha participated in the first coming of Christ, as a source streaming into the enlightened astral body of Jesus of Nazareth,[13] so, too, does he serve to assist the enlightenment of humanity at this time of the Second Coming, working in union with Christ. The life energy of those choosing to open themselves to this influx of grace will be infused with the fire of spirit—as they receive the power of the good that will usher forth in the teachings of Gautama's successor.

In appendix 1, Powell quotes extensively from Steiner's two lectures *The Spiritual Bells of Easter*, wherein the mysteries of the East meet the mysteries of the West. In these lectures we read about the future mission of the successor of Gautama Buddha, the bodhisattva who will become the Maitreya Buddha, as the one who, from the forces that live within the core of the human being's own nature, will be capable of redeeming the physical body. Prophetic legend depicts that the Maitreya Buddha will perform a miraculous act in relation to the mysteriously preserved body of Kashyapa. This event, as Steiner indicates, will occur in the fire of the blood that dwells within the human physical body, into which the Mystery of Golgotha planted a seed as Christ resurrected on Easter morning.[14] Shortly after the coming of the Maitreya Buddha in approximately 4443, this great individuality will reveal something of the mystery associated with Christ—that

---

13 Steiner, *Esoteric Christianity and the Mission of Christian Rosenkreutz*, lecture 7; see quotation, page xiv.

14 See appendix I in this book for extensive excerpts from Rudolf Steiner's lectures *The Spiritual Bells of Easter*: "Thus, although through the spiritualization of his breath he had made his body incorruptible, even Kashyapa with his supreme enlightenment could not yet find complete redemption. The incorruptible body must wait in the secret cave until it is drawn forth by the Maitreya Buddha. Only when the 'I' has spiritualized the physical body to such a degree that the Christ Impulse streams into the physical body, is the miraculous cosmic fire no longer needed for redemption; for redemption is now brought about by the fire quickened in our own inner being, in the blood. Thus the radiance streaming from the Mystery of Golgotha is also able to shed light on a legend as wonderful and profound as that of Kashyapa."

of the overcoming of death, when, according to the legend Steiner mentioned, the Maitreya Buddha touches with his right hand, in union with the spiritualized fire of the future, the incorruptible body of Kashyapa, Gautama Buddha's appointed successor.

It is predictable enough that the dawning revival of Buddhism at the commencement of the unfolding of this new six-hundred-year cultural wave will most likely be spearheaded—whether working in the public arena or from behind the scenes—by the successor of Gautama Buddha, the bodhisattva who will become the Maitreya Buddha. This successor, as indicated in this book, is the one who brings a renewal of religion and is capable of leading each willing soul to the source of a newly forming community spirit. This is the antidote to the suffocating breath of evil.

Powell reminds us that only by maintaining freedom will humanity have the ability to choose between Christ and Antichrist. Apathy, indifference, and ignorance will deliver human beings into the imprisonment heralded by the dragon's unholy breath, which is the inversion of the Christ-breath that raised Lazarus from the grave. Powell gives notice, pointing to a future that is in certain respects upon us even now. In so doing, he is acting in the spirit of the magi tradition wherein the future is seen and humanity is thus prepared—but only if they can hear the truth and discern new octaves in spiritual guidance. He points to a bodhisattva incarnational lineage: Abraham, Kashyapa, Jeshu ben Pandira, and Maitreya. Moreover, as in the story of the magi or three kings, an ancient text tells a story that points the way, through the movement of the stars, to humanity's collective destiny.

July 27, 2014 is a date that emerges from the cosmic indications of this ancient prophecy as a likely possibility for this event. If this dating is correct, it is the time when the "bearer of goodness"—also known as the "teacher of righteousness"—is prophesied to manifest in earthly incarnation in concordance with a particular heavenly configuration: a conjunction of Jupiter with the New Moon (conjunction of the Sun and the Moon) occurring in the region of the constellation of Cancer containing the beautiful star cluster Praesepe (the Beehive), the region known in Vedic astrology as the *nakshatra Pushya*. This may indeed be the sign in the heavens that has long been awaited. Powell is directing us to the events marking the fruition of what Steiner indicated. The mystery continues to unfold through the continuity between the research of Steiner and that of Powell.

Powell also draws attention to the period of 3½ years, spoken of in chapter 13 of the Book of Revelation, as marking the reign of the "beast"—known in Christian tradition as the Antichrist. He indicates that the 3½ years appears to have already commenced in June 2013, around the time when the striving for a global surveillance state became publicly revealed.[15] At the end of chapter 1, he outlines the effect these years will have and the unique challenge that each of the three years (2014, 2015, 2016) will bring. To be forewarned is to be well armed. As part of the challenge of this time, he gives the image of the disciples at the Ascension, when they stood bereft as Christ ascended beyond them.

It was in the agony of their loss that a new organ of cognition was formed among them. They became a community that was, is, and ever shall be representative of the community of Eternal Israel—this being a name for the community of disciples of the Etheric Christ and of Christ's future manifestations at different ascending levels of being. The prophets who led to forming the community of Ancient Israel are surely with us again, some undoubtedly leading us to the revelations of the Messiah in this

---

15 The existence of the global surveillance program first became revealed by the Guardian and the Washington Post on June 6, 2013, but the far-reaching extent of this surveillance—that the program allows analysts to search with no prior authorization through vast databases containing emails, online chats, and the browsing histories of millions of individuals—only became known later. Powell focuses upon June 19, 2013, as a crucial date here (see chapter 1).

time of the Second Coming.[16] Unimaginable consequences will result if this crucial time goes by unnoticed. The new Pentecost, says Powell, will be when every eye shall behold Christ in the etheric.[17] Hearts will then be pierced with his unspeakable glory. Hence, it is time to prepare for this event signifying the "greatest mystery of our time."[18]

The moral courage of those who stand undaunted by the magnitude of the task at hand can serve as an indispensable contribution in helping to prevent Ahriman's victory in the great struggle that is now unfolding. This is a struggle for every human soul and for the whole Earth, in which the existential choice is to unite with the Etheric Christ on the path of spiritual evolution leading ultimately to the resurrection, or to become subject to Ahriman and thereby become a slave in his dark kingdom.

---

16   Steiner, *The Reappearance of Christ in the Etheric*, p. 21: "Those who lived at one time on Earth as Moses, Abraham, and other prophets will again be recognizable to human beings.... All those who prepared the way for him will be recognized in a new way by those who have experienced the new Christ event."

17   Steiner, *From Jesus to Christ*, p. 46: "An event of profound significance will take place in the etheric world. And the occurrence of this event, an event connected with Christ himself, will make it possible for human beings to learn to see Christ, to look upon him." In this connection, see also Andreev, *The Rose of the World*, p. 342: "The Second Coming is to occur simultaneously at a multitude of points on Earth...so that every single being will have seen and heard him. In other words, the Planetary Logos is to attain the inconceivable power to materialize simultaneously in as many places as there will then be consciousnesses to perceive him...so that all peoples and nations on Earth will see 'the Son of Man coming on the clouds of heaven.'" See also Andreev, "Rosa Mira: The Rose of the World" (tr. by R.P. in *Prophecy–Phenomena–Hope*, p. 89: "Christ will take on as many forms as there are consciousnesses on Earth to behold him. He will adapt himself to everyone, and will converse with all. His forms, in an unimaginable way, will simultaneously yield an image: One who appears in heaven surrounded by unspeakable glory. There will not be a single being on Earth who will not see the Son of God and hear his Word."

18   Steiner, *The Reappearance of Christ in the Etheric*, p. 19: "The greatest mystery of our time concerns the Second Coming of Christ...People will be able to see the etheric body of Christ; humankind will grow into a world where the Christ will be visible to newly awakened faculties."

Through the endeavors of certain spiritual teachers, many are becoming aware of the presence of the Etheric Christ and the teachings of the Maitreya–Kalki individuality, signifying the beginning of a new paradigm in world history. Just as humanity's guiding spiritual powers sent the great prophet Mani, the founder of Manichaeism, into incarnation at the beginning of the Piscean Age in AD 215 to seed unity in religions (which he did on his journeys far and wide), so do the guiding spirits send their messengers at each new beginning of the six-hundred-year cultural rhythm. We now find ourselves on the doorstep of yet another new cultural wave in 2014, 1,800 years (3 x 600 years) after Mani's birth at the start of the six-hundred-year cultural wave that commenced at the beginning of the Age of Pisces.

❀

The prophesied return of the being awaited as the Maitreya in Buddhist tradition and as Kalki in Hinduism is founded upon the two complementary streams of influence working together. These unite the descending spiritual grace from above and the rigorous inner effort creating an ascent from below. This interweaving is what Valentin Tomberg describes as "two contrasting forces acting simultaneously."[19] The loftiest manifestation of such a union of two forces is exemplified in the mystery of the two Jesus children.[20] In this case, it was the angelic Nathan Jesus from above and the

---

19   See appendix 2 of this book.

20   Steiner pointed out that the child Jesus visited by the magi (whose birth is described in the Matthew gospel) and the child Jesus visited by the shepherds (whose birth is described in the Luke gospel) had different genealogies and were, in fact, separate and different individuals. To distinguish between these two, he referred to the former as the "Solomon Jesus," since his genealogy descends from King Solomon and he was very wise, and he referred to the latter as the "Nathan Jesus," since his genealogy descends from David's son Nathan. The "Nathan Jesus" child was exceptionally pure; he was by nature angelic. For an overview of Rudolf Steiner's research regarding the "two Jesus children," see Robert Powell, *Chronicle of the Living Christ*.

wisdom-filled Solomon Jesus from below working together. The two created the perfection of a hermetic union that prepared the way for the incarnation of the Son of God. This uniting of two spiritual forces is reflected in the Kalki–Maitreya mystery; for as these two complementary actions come together, a bodhisattva reaches buddhahood.

This union can occur at different levels; yet wherever the continuity between ascent and descent coincide, there is a union between the human and the divine. This is true hermeticism:

> The father thereof is the Sun, the mother the Moon.
> The wind carried it in its womb; the earth is the nurse thereof.
> It is the father of all works of wonder (*thelema*) throughout the whole world.
> The power thereof is perfect, if it be cast on to Earth.
> It will separate the element of earth from that of fire, the subtle from the gross, gently and with great sagacity.
> It doth ascend from earth to heaven.
> Again it doth descend to earth, and uniteth in itself the force from things superior and things inferior.[21]

The year 2014 may well signify the end of humanity's long exile from the descending revelatory stream of guidance. To meet these changing times, however, the effects of materialism must be overcome. An ahrimanic web of lies and deceit, filled with illusory assumptions, has woven itself around us individually as well as around our entire globe. This has effectively dulled receptivity to the extraordinary spiritual realities that are unfolding before us. So long as the presence of this dark web goes unnoticed, one lives within its influence and cannot become independent in one's own being. Recognition of this condition allows for objective experience that frees the soul to perceive hitherto unforeseen forces

---

21   Emerald Table of Hermes Trismegistus as quoted in Anonymous, *Meditations on the Tarot: A Journey into Christian Hermeticism*, pp. 25 and 607.

in action. As independence is achieved, a path of understanding opens before us and the teachings of the Maitreya–Kalki individuality can serve as a guide. Each one of us must actively choose to nurture our individual awakening if we are to realize the absolute sovereignty of our innermost being.

Steiner inaugurated a path of spiritual awakening when he became leader of the German Section of the Theosophical Society. The first decade of his leadership as an esoteric teacher was a time when he was writing his fundamental books, giving his "early" courses of lectures, as well as introducing his mystery plays with the first one in 1910. In 1912 to 1913, he parted from the Theosophical Society and founded the Anthroposophical Society. Now, one hundred years later, the continuous succession of spiritual guidance has reached a new octave, one that is crucial in helping us meet the approaching trials. Wakefulness is essential—indeed, a necessity. A tear occurred between East and West with the separation of Steiner from the Theosophical Society. This wound must now be healed to provide a new basis for understanding the magnitude of miracles[22] that are unfolding before us.

The collaboration of Powell and Isaacson weaves a coat of many colors, revealing the esoteric significance of 2014 in its many layers of meaning. Dr. Powell outlines the signs of the times, and Estelle Isaacson shares revelatory visions through which the words of the Buddha's successor lead us to an experience of his presence.[23] Those who find him will not falter under the weight of fear in all its many disguises, nor will they engage in the false

---

22 Ibid., p. 67: "Yes, the miraculous does exist, for life is only a series of miracles, if we understand by 'miracle' not the absence of cause…but rather the visible effect of an invisible cause, or the effect on a lower plane due to a cause on a higher plane."

23 The concentration of thought presented in chapter 1 of this book cannot be avoided, so vast and momentous are the ideas Powell presents. Some may find it easier to read the visions of Isaacson first (in chapters 2 to 7), and thereafter return to read chapter 1.

spirit of compromise that renders distortion to the true light of the world, which we can now behold. Together these authors illumine a path that can be taken by many—a path leading to the recognition that the continuation of the dark age of Kali Yuga beyond its appointed time is coming to a close, and a new age of light and truth (Satya Yuga) is now beginning.

2014 AND THE COMING OF THE KALKI AVATAR

A new six-hundred-year cultural rhythm is due to begin in the year 2014. This coincides with the prophesied date of the coming of a great leader of humanity, Kalki Avatar.[1] Kalki is awaited in Hinduism as the coming avatar—after Rama, Krishna, and Buddha or Balarama (the brother of Krishna), who are regarded as the seventh, eighth, and ninth avatars. In the Hindu tradition Kalki (also Kalkin or Kalaki) is the name of the tenth and final avatar of Vishnu, the Maintainer, the second Person of the Hindu *Trimurti*, corresponding to the Son in the Holy Trinity. The prophecy quoted below indicates that Kalki will come at the end of *Kali Yuga*. The name Kalki denotes the *Annihilator of Ignorance*. He is said to be the ruler of the realm of Shambhala, the lost paradise at the heart of Mother Earth.[2] Through Kalki as his avatar, Vishnu will descend to annihilate ignorance and restore the golden age of virtue, *Satya Yuga*. It is imagined that he will come on a white horse, wielding a flaming sword with which to destroy wickedness and restore righteousness to the earth. His is a two-edged sword—for the good, and against evil. The description of the Kalki Avatar aligns remarkably with that of the Maitreya Buddha (*Maitreya,*

---

1   Powell, "Subnature and the Second Coming," *The Inner Life of the Earth*, pp. 116–118. The emergence of the true Kalki Avatar in 2014 is being preempted from various quarters—one example being Sri Kalki Bhagavan, the self-styled "Living Avatar."

2   Concerning Shambhala, see Robert Powell, *Cultivating Inner Radiance and the Body of Immortality*, pp. 26–27, 146–148, 167.

"bearer of goodness"), the successor of Gautama Buddha, who is awaited in the Buddhist tradition.[3]

The source for the prophecy of the coming of the Kalki Avatar is the *S'rîmad Bhâgavatam* (also known as the *Bhâgavata Purâna*), which is one of the most important sacred books of India. It is arranged in twelve so-called cantos, and comprises 335 chapters with a total of about 18,000 verses. It stresses the prime importance of the *maintaining* aspect of God personified by the transcendental form of *Vishnu*. According to tradition, the writer of this work was Vyâsadeva (Vyâsa), also known as Bâdarâyana. He is said to have compiled the Vedas and the great epic poem entitled the *Mahâbhârata*, of which the *Bhagavad Gîta* is the most important part. Vyâsa also wrote the Purânas as well as the *Brahma-sûtra*.

Given this, one possible date forecast for the emergence of the Kalki Avatar as the bearer of a new and mighty impulse for the evolution of the Earth and humanity is July 27, 2014 (see below). This coincides, within twenty months, with the date of the end of the Maya calendar on December 21, 2012. Consequently—bearing in mind the elucidation in chapter 6 of *Christ & the Maya Calendar* (on dating *Kali Yuga* in relation to the Maya Calendar,[4] whereby the beginning of the transition (from a "modified Hindu perspective") of the *Kali Yuga* ("Dark Age") to the New Age of *Satya Yuga* ("Age of Light") is equated with December 21, 2012— it seems fitting to look at the prophecy concerning the coming of the Kalki Avatar. The Kalki Avatar, like Christ, is a bearer of the Mystery of Love.

---

3   Anonymous, *Meditations on the Tarot*, p. 614: "Since it is a question of the work of the fusion of revelation and knowledge, of spirituality and intellectuality, it is a matter throughout of the fusion of the avatar principle with the Buddha principle. In other words, the Kalki Avatar awaited by the Hindus and the Maitreya Buddha awaited by the Buddhists will manifest in a single personality. On the historical plane the Maitreya Buddha and the Kalki Avatar will be one."

4   Powell and Dann, *Christ and the Maya Calendar*, chapter 6.

When the Supreme Lord has appeared on earth as Kalki, the maintainer of religion, *Satya Yuga* will begin, and human society will bring forth progeny in the mode of goodness.... When the Moon, the Sun, and Brhaspati (Jupiter) are together in the constellation Karkata (Cancer), and all three enter simultaneously into the lunar mansion Pushya—at that exact moment the age of *Satya*, or *Krita*, will begin. (*S'rîmad Bhâgavatam* 12.2: 22, 24)

Thus, when the Sun, Moon, and Jupiter are in conjunction in the Hindu lunar *nakshatra Pushya* (4°–17° Cancer in the sidereal zodiac), the emergence of the Kalki Avatar, the "bearer of goodness," is expected. It is in this lunar mansion that the beautiful star cluster known as the Beehive (Greek: *Praesepe*), Jupiter's place of exaltation, is to be found.[5] Evidently the Hindu sages attributed something special to Jupiter's location in this part of the zodiac: a special impulse of the Good comes to expression here.

One historical possibility of this conjunction, the prophesied conjunction of the Sun, Moon, and Jupiter in Pushya, will take place on July 27, 2014—shortly after what could possibly be designated as the start of the historical 3½ years of the earthly rule of the Antichrist—also known as the time of the "incarnation of Ahriman" (see later, "The 3½ Years"). If it is indeed true that this rule, denoted by the incarnation of Ahriman into his human vessel (Mr. X), began around the summer solstice of 2013, it follows that the 3½ years of Antichrist's reign as world ruler is expected to end shortly after the winter solstice of 2016, in which case the emergence of the Kalki Avatar during this 3½-year period assumes extraordinary significance. Against this background, the conjunction on July 27, 2014, may signify the emergence of the Kalki Avatar to inaugurate a new spiritual era when something of the

---

5   The exact location of Praesepe, which denotes the place of exaltation of Jupiter in the zodiac, is 12°39' Cancer—see Powell and Bowden, *Astrogeographia: Correspondences between the Stars and Earthly Locations*, pp. 35–41.

impulse of goodness, connected with the work of the Kalki Avatar, might be expected to begin to stream in as a counterbalance to the evil of the Antichrist. For the Kalki Avatar is the teacher of morality (goodness) and is the chosen vessel for the second Person of the Godhead (Vishnu in the Hindu tradition; Christ in the Christian tradition) to spearhead the overcoming of the evil of the Antichrist. The Kalki Avatar's possible emergence in 2014 could manifest in a new spiritual impulse along the lines of strengthening moral consciousness, empowering deeds of sacred magic, as indicated in the quote later in this article from *S'rîmad Bhâgavatam* 12.2: 16–23. The Kalki Avatar, also known as the "maintainer of religion," works in particular with sacred magic for the renewal of true religion.

Against a background of astrosophical research, as mentioned above, the potential advent of the Maitreya Buddha/Kalki Avatar individuality[6] in 2014 coincides with an indication by Rudolf Steiner in connection with the six-hundred-year rhythm of culture. This rhythm (as discussed in *Hermetic Astrology,* volume I) is actually the half-rhythm of the 1,199-year Venus rhythm, the time it takes for the "Venus pentagram" to rotate once (moving retrograde) through all twelve signs of the sidereal zodiac.[7] This period of almost exactly twelve hundred years is the length of time that elapses between the start of a new zodiacal age and the beginning of the new cultural epoch corresponding to that age. For example,

---

6   As indicated in footnote 3, "On the historical plane the Maitreya Buddha and the Kalki Avatar will be one." As I have described in *Hermetic Astrology,* vol. I, following the indications of Steiner, the bodhisattva known as the Maitreya individuality generally incarnates once every century and will continue to do so for about 2,500 years, until around the year 4443, when he will incarnate as the Maitreya Buddha. This is the approximate date, then, that is referred to in the statement, "On the historical plane the Maitreya Buddha and the Kalki Avatar will be one." Thus, in speaking of the Maitreya Buddha–Kalki Avatar individuality, it is a matter of the bodhisattva who will become the Maitreya Buddha–Kalki Avatar.

7   Powell, *Hermetic Astrology,* vol. 1, pp. 58–66. This edition (available from Amazon.com) is a reprint of the 1987 edition; see chapter 3.

the *Age of Pisces*, which began when the vernal point on account of the *precession of the equinoxes* shifted retrograde from Aries into Pisces, started in the year 215, reckoned to be the birth year of the Prophet Mani, the founder of Manichaeism. In 1414 (1,199 years later), the corresponding *Piscean cultural epoch* commenced, birthing the Renaissance in Europe. It is striking that the great individuality of Joan of Arc, who was born in 1412 (immediately preceding this date of 1414), emerged near the beginning of the new cultural epoch as a leading figure in the shaping of the unfolding new epoch, the fifth since the destruction of Atlantis. Looking at the half-period, going back six hundred years from 1414, we arrive at 814, the year of Charlemagne's death,[8] and the beginning of a new era in Europe, when the monastic schools started to flourish. Going forward six hundred years from 1414, we reach 2014—the present time. Concerning this date of 2014, Rudolf Steiner indicated prophetically in 1911, "We are living today at the beginning of a period of transition before the onset of the next six-hundred-year *wave of culture*, when something *entirely new* is pressing in upon us, when the Christ impulse is to be enriched by something new."[9]

Here it is clear that six hundred years is the half period of the 1,199-year rhythm of the Venus pentagram. Steiner describes the six-hundred-year period as a *cultural wave*. Evidently, two *cultural waves*, each six-hundred years long, elapse between the beginning of a zodiacal age and the start of the corresponding cultural epoch.

Applied to the Piscean Age, the first cultural wave of six hundred years was from 215 to 814, the year of the death of

---

8   The year 814 was also the start of the period of the Archangel Raphael (814–1169) connected with the 355-year rhythm of the planet Mercury; this was the time of founding the Mysteries of the Holy Grail associated with Parzival, whom Steiner connects with the time of Charlemagne.

9   Steiner, *Background to the Gospel of St. Mark,* p. 153 (italics added by R.P.).

Charlemagne (Carolingian Renaissance), and the second cultural wave of six hundred years lasted from 814 to 1414 (flourishing of the monastic schools in Europe). Adding another six hundred years, we arrive at 2014 as the start of a new cultural wave.

Given that 2014 begins a new six-hundred-year cultural wave, it is possible that a spiritual leader such as the Kalki Avatar could emerge at this time as a bearer of the impulse for the new wave of culture as a seed impulse for the next six hundred years. It is a matter of a new culture being seeded during this challenging time of the reign of the Antichrist and his False Prophet. However, that reign will come to an end, as Rudolf Steiner indicates in his discussion of "the fall of the Beast and of the False Prophet."[10] As mentioned above, one possibility is that "the fall of the Beast"—i.e., the end of the reign of the Antichrist—will be shortly after the winter solstice of 2016.

This is further elucidated in connection with the thesis developed in Chapter 6 of *Christ & the Maya Calendar*.[11] Although, according to Rudolf Steiner, the *Kali Yuga* ended and the *Satya Yuga* ("New Age of Light") began in 1899, evidently there was a 113-year transition period until the end of the Maya calendar in 2012, so that the full flowering of the New Age, *Satya Yuga*, only truly began around the time of the winter solstice of the year 2012. The coming of the Kalki Avatar in 2014 could thus be seen as fulfilling the inauguration of this New Age. In this light, let us consider the following words by way of attunement to the prophecy of the activity of the Kalki Avatar in our time as the transmitter of the power of goodness that our modern world is in need of now, more than ever before:

> By the time the age of *Kali* ends…religious principles will be ruined…so-called religion will be mostly atheistic…the occupations of men will be stealing, lying and needless

---

10   Steiner, *The Book of Revelation and the Work of the Priest*, pp. 154–156.

11   Powell and Dann, *Christ and the Maya Calendar*.

violence, and all the social classes will be reduced to the lowest level.... Family ties will extend no further than the immediate bonds of marriage...homes will be devoid of piety, and all human beings will have become like asses. At that time, the Supreme personality of the Godhead will appear on the earth. Acting with the power of pure spiritual goodness, he will rescue eternal religion.... Lord Kalki will appear in...the great soul of *Vishnuyasha*.[12]... When the Supreme Lord has appeared on earth as Kalki, the maintainer of religion, *Satya Yuga* will begin, and human society will bring forth progeny in the mode of goodness. (*S'rîmad Bhâgavatam* 12; 2; 16–23)

Steiner spoke of the beginning of the Satya Yuga in 1899.[13] He knew that the ancient Hindu texts foresaw that the full flowering of the Satya Yuga was far in the future.[14] Yet, he also realized that the influences of the Satya Yuga would begin streaming in at the

---

12   *Vishnuyasha* is the Hindu name in the *S'rîmad Bhâgavatam* for the human being who will be the bearer of the Kalki Avatar, and for the Kalki Avatar to emerge in the year 2014, it follows that *Vishnuyasha* must already be in incarnation.

13   Steiner, *The Reappearance of Christ in the Etheric;* chapter 6, "The Sermon on the Mount and the Land of Shambhala," Munich, March 15, 1910 (pp. 99–100): "Kali Yuga, however, continued until 1899. This was a particularly important year in human evolution, because it marked the end of the 5,000-year period of Kali Yuga and the beginning of a new stage in human evolution. In addition to the old faculties present during Kali Yuga, humankind would now develop new spiritual faculties. Thus we are approaching a period when new natural faculties and possibilities for looking into the divine spirit worlds will awaken. Before the first half of the twentieth century has passed, some people will, with full I-awareness, witness the penetration of the divine spirit world into the physical sensory world, just as Saul did during his transformation into Paul near Damascus. This will become the normal condition for some people." Note by R.P.: It is remarkable, against this background, how in our time the city of Damascus has come into the forefront of human consciousness—in a way, however, that obscures the spiritual significance of the event of Paul's transformation near Damascus as an archetype for the encounter with Christ in the etheric realm.

14   For a reconciliation between the traditional Hindu dates concerning the end of Kali Yuga and the start of Satya Yuga (also known as Krita Yuga, the Age of Truth, the Golden Age), see Powell and Dann, *Christ and the Maya Calendar;* chapter 6, "Dating Kali Yuga in Relation to the Maya Calendar"; and chapter 2, pp. 28–33, "Krishna and the Kali Yuga."

start of what he called the "New Age of Light," a time when the Kali Yuga would have reached its culmination some twenty years after the commencement of the reign of the Archangel Michael in 1879.[15] From the start of the New Age (in 1899) onward, further manifestations of the Kali Yuga would become increasingly degenerate. Rudolf Steiner foresaw that a new turning point would enter human consciousness around 1933—the approximate time of the onset of Christ's coming in the etheric realm. From this point onward, time would be nourished increasingly by what is radiating from the future—i.e., from the future that the Etheric Christ is leading us toward—this transition marking the spiritual renewal of the clairvoyance natural in human souls, a transition bringing "momentous consequences":

---

15 The Age of Michael started, according to Steiner, in 1879, as the beginning of the reign of the Archangel Michael—one of seven ages ruled by seven different Archangels in a particular sequence, each age lasting 355 years, so that the total of seven ages lasts for 2485 years, and then the sequence is repeated again. The Age of Michael is particularly significant, as the age in which the confrontation with the Dragon (Ahriman) takes place; for this is the signature of the present time, bearing in mind Rudolf Steiner's indication that "before only a part of the third millennium of the post-Christian era has elapsed, there will be in the West an actual incarnation of Ahriman—Ahriman in the flesh," *The Incarnation of Ahriman*, p. 37. Interestingly, the end of the present Age of Michael coincides with the date of the alignment of our Sun at the winter solstice with the center of the Milky Way Galaxy, in the year 2234, which marks the end of the Age of Michael (1879–2234). The Age of Michael is the current archangelic period for humanity and the Earth, which will culminate with the alignment of our Sun with the Central Sun (galactic center) at the winter solstice. The archangelic periods, each 355 sidereal years in length, are a succession of historical periods in which, during each period, one of seven Archangels, in succession, assumes the task of guiding humanity and the Earth: Michael/Sun (607–152 BC); Oriphiel/Saturn (152 BC–AD 204); Anael/Venus (204–459); Zachariel/Jupiter (459–814); Raphael/Mercury (814–1169); Samael/Mars (1169–1524); Gabriel/Moon (1524–1879); and Michael/Sun (1879–2234). The 355-year period is associated with the planet Mercury, during which Mercury completes 1,474 orbits of the Sun and, simultaneously, 1,119 synodic periods (orbits of the Earth). See Steiner, *From the History and Contents of the First Section of the Esoteric School, 1904–1914*, in which he refers to the archangelic periods, though without giving a precise dating.

The course of the evolution of humanity is such that from our time onward a renaissance of the Abraham epoch will take place as we pass slowly into the third millennium. In pre-Christian times, the sequence was Abraham epoch, Moses epoch, Solomon epoch. In the Christian era the order is reversed: Solomon epoch, Moses epoch, Abraham epoch. We are moving toward the Abraham epoch, and this will inevitably bring momentous consequences in its train. [According to Rudolf Steiner, since the year 2000, the start of the third millennium, we are already in the Abraham epoch.]

Let us recall what was of essential significance in the pre-Christian Abraham epoch. It was the fact that the old clairvoyance had disappeared, that there had been bestowed upon the human being a consciousness of the Divine closely bound up with human faculties. Everything that humanity could acquire from this brain-bound consciousness of the Divine had by now been gradually exhausted and there is very little left to be gained through these faculties. But on the other hand, in the new Abraham epoch exactly the opposite path is taken—the path which leads humanity away from vision confined to the physical and material, away from intellectual inferences based upon material data. We are moving along the path leading into the regions where human beings once dwelt in times before the Abraham epoch. It is the path that will make states of natural clairvoyance possible for human beings, states in which natural clairvoyant forces will be in active operation.

During Kali Yuga itself, initiation alone could lead into the spiritual worlds in the right way. Initiation does, of course, lead to higher stages that will be accessible to human beings only in the far-distant future. However, the first signs of a natural faculty of clairvoyance will become evident fairly soon, as the renewal of the Abraham epoch approaches.

Thus, after human beings have acquired "I"-consciousness, after they have come to know the "I" as a firm inner center, they are led out of themselves again in order to be able to look with an even deeper vision into the spiritual worlds. The ending of Kali Yuga has to do with this also. Having lasted for five thousand years, Kali Yuga ended in AD 1899. This was a year of crucial importance for the evolution of humanity. Naturally, it is again an approximate date, for things happen gradually. [Note added by R.P.: According to Rudolf Steiner, Kali Yuga lasted for five thousand years, having begun in the year -3101. Adding 1899 and 3101 is 5,000.] Just as the year 3101 BC can be indicated as a point of time when humanity was led down from the stage of the old clairvoyance to physical vision and intellectuality, so the year 1899 is the time when humanity received an impetus toward the first beginnings of a future clairvoyance. And it is the lot of humankind, already in this twentieth century before the next millennium—indeed for a few individuals in the first half of this [twentieth] century—to develop the first rudiments of a new faculty of clairvoyance that quite certainly will appear if human beings prove capable of understanding it. It must be realized, however, that there are two possibilities. It belongs to the very essence of the human soul that natural faculties of clairvoyance will arise in the future in a few people during the first half of the twentieth century, and in more and more human beings during the next two thousand five hundred years, until finally there will be a sufficient number who, if they so desire, will have the new, natural clairvoyance. A distinction must be made, of course, between cultivated and natural clairvoyance.[16]

Let us return now to consider the identity of the Kalki Avatar/Maitreya Buddha individuality. When he was asked if he was the Maitreya Bodhisattva individuality,[17] whom he had spoken of as having been incarnated on the Earth about one hundred years before Christ as Jeshu ben Pandira, the teacher

---

16 Steiner, *The Reappearance of Christ in the Etheric*, chapter 5, "The Reappearance of Christ in the Etheric," Stuttgart, March 6, 1910, pp. 78–80 [translation revised by R.P.].

17 According to Steiner, the Maitreya Bodhisattva individuality, as the successor to Gautama Buddha, incarnates in almost every century by way of preparation for his final, culminating incarnation as the Maitreya Buddha in about 2,500 years (see footnote 6).

Birth of Kalki Avatar - Geocentric
At London, United Kingdom, Latitude 51N30', Longitude 0W10'
Date: Sunday, 27/JUL/2014, Gregorian
Time: 0: 0, Time Zone GMD
Sidereal Time 19:17:34, Vernal Point 5 ♓ 3'24", House System: Placidus
Zodiac: Sidereal SVP, Aspect set: Conjunction/Square/Opposition

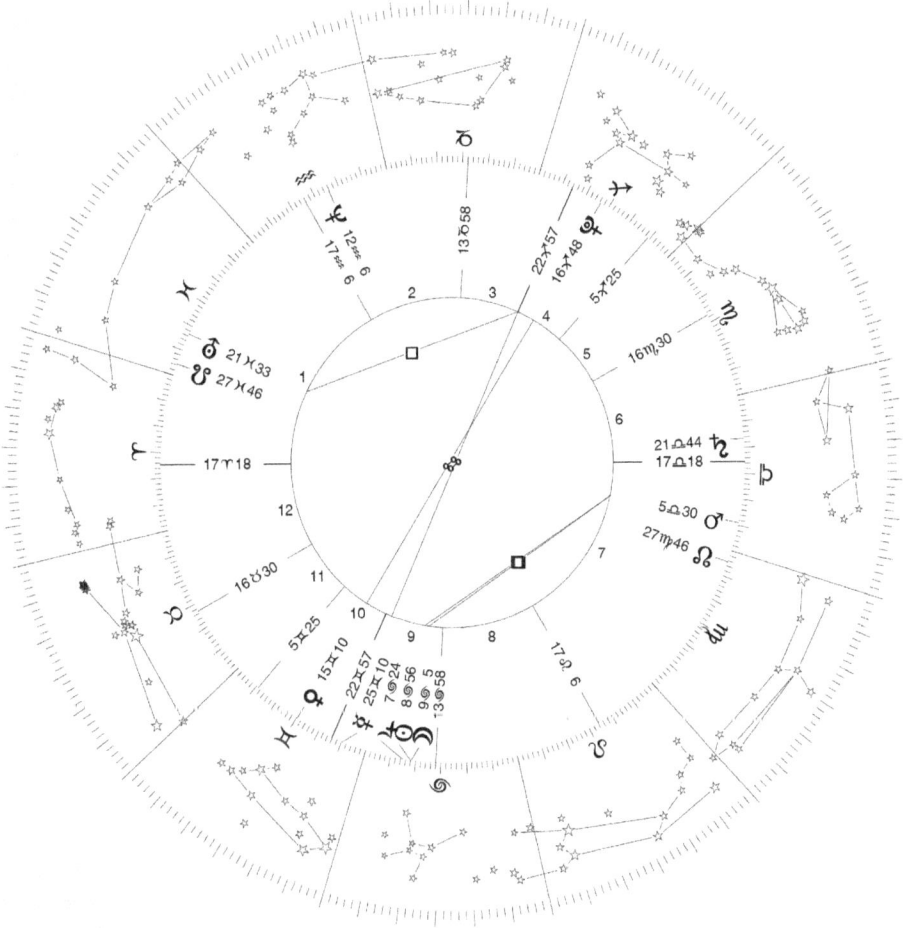

of the Essenes, Rudolf Steiner replied that he was not—and
that he had no connection with Jeshu ben Pandira, meaning
that he (Rudolf Steiner) had not been incarnated as Jeshu ben
Pandira.[18] Moreover, Steiner deflected attention from himself as

18   In footnote 155, page 169 of Meyer and Vreede, *The Bodhisattva
      Question*, Meyer notes that Walter Vegelahn (1880–1959) was one of the
      stenographers who recorded more than 500 lectures of Steiner from 1903
      on. Among these was the Berne cycle, *According to Matthew*. Shortly

a bodhisattva by pointing to the bodhisattva who would come after him, whom he said would be the *actual herald of Christ in his etheric form*.[19] Steiner indicated that this bodhisattva incarnated at the "beginning of the century"—signifying the beginning of the twentieth century—and he also indicated that this bodhisattva would emerge ("become noticeable") in the 1930s.[20] It is also reportedly said that this bodhisattva would be connected with the Anthroposophical Society and that one would be able to recognize him by the fact that he would speak of the return of Christ in the etheric. These indications offer a few pointers concerning the identity of this bodhisattva.[21]

---

before his death [in 1959] he made the following statement, in October 1958, to a visitor in Berlin: "It was in Berne that Rudolf Steiner spoke about the Bodhisattva. The members were curious to know whom Dr. Steiner had in mind with this statement. They put their heads together and chose the most suitable among them, Günther Wagner, to approach Dr. Steiner about it. Steiner's answer was: 'I am not the one.' At the following meeting, Dr. Steiner gave a report of all that had happened during the previous months and mentioned also the Berne lectures. While doing so he interrupted what he was saying by an aside: 'I wish to add in parentheses to all those who are ever ready to invent incarnations from their fantasy, that in my own individuality I have no connection with Jeshu ben Pandira.'" The communication of this important fact (from a member of the Rudolf Steiner *Nachlassverwaltung* [literary estate administration]) was given to the author [Thomas Meyer] by the person who received it, to whom he is very grateful. (Words in brackets [ ] added by R.P.)

19   Steiner emphasized that Jeshu ben Pandira reincarnated in the twentieth century as a great Bodhisattva individuality in order to fulfill the lofty mission of proclaiming Christ's coming in the etheric realm, beginning around 1933. In Steiner's own words on the reincarnation of the Bodhisattva Jeshu ben Pandira in the twentieth century, *"He will be the actual herald of Christ in his etheric form"* (lecture on Jeshu ben Pandira, Leipzig, Nov. 4, 1911; see footnote 13 in appendix 1, page 88).

20   Powell, "Rudolf Steiner, Valentin Tomberg, and the Return of Christ in the Etheric" (www.sophiafoundation.org/articles). My research indicates that the emergence of this bodhisattva individuality began around 1933.

21   Powell, "Valentin Tomberg Symposium 2009 Report: Valentin Tomberg and the Bodhisattva of the 20th Century" (www.sophiafoundation.org/articles).

Furthermore, Rudolf Steiner wrote toward the end of his life about his "possible successor," whom, however, he never named, because he died before the time had come when he would have been able to do so.[22] It is important to understand that when he used the expression *successor*, this was by no means an arbitrary term. He was using it in a very specific way, as it is used in the bodhisattva circle—for example, when Gautama Buddha pointed to Kashyapa as his successor, thus indicating that he would be the next Buddha, the Maitreya Buddha. The term *successor* has a very specific meaning in the bodhisattva circle. When Rudolf Steiner used that expression, he was speaking as a bodhisattva— one of the circle of the great teachers of humanity—who was going to name his "possible successor." But that was not possible because of Rudolf Steiner's premature death. Nevertheless, this important indication implies that this bodhisattva—the successor of Rudolf Steiner—is the one who on the one hand was destined to proclaim from 1933 onward the event of Christ's coming in an etheric form and on the other hand who in about 2,500 years time will become the next Buddha, the Maitreya Buddha, referred to as the *Bearer of the Good*.

It was Steiner's mission as a bodhisattva[23] to bring *spiritual science*—i.e., to bring the great spiritual truths of existence to expression for our present-day culture. For a deeper level of understanding, *truth* is the mission of science as a whole. However, as Rudolf Steiner pointed out, science has unfortunately become taken hold of—not universally, but by and large, at least to a

---

22   Steiner used this expression when he formulated Statute 7 of the Anthroposophical Society: "The establishment of the School of Spiritual Science is, to begin with, in the hands of Rudolf Steiner, who will appoint his collaborators and his possible successor" (from a pamphlet by the Anthroposophical Society in Great Britain; London, 1925).

23   That Steiner was an incarnation of a great bodhisattva individuality, one of the twelve great teachers of humanity, is *absolutely certain*, as I will show, based on statements by Steiner himself, in a forthcoming publication. Within the bodhisattva circle, Steiner occupies a very special position at the "right hand" of Christ.

certain extent—by dark forces, thus becoming a vehicle for the permeation of our culture and civilization with untruths about the human being and the world. One example of such an untruth or inverted idea—one that is widespread and widely believed—is the Darwinian thesis that human beings are descended from the apes, when in reality human beings are a class of beings unto themselves, and therefore the "missing link" will never be found, because there is no "missing link" between apes and human beings.[24] Many other examples of this kind of untruth put forward with conviction by modern science could be given.

Rudolf Steiner's mission was to work in the scientific field—expanding upon it—to bring for humankind the truths about the human being's true spiritual nature and spiritual origin, including how to apply these truths in practical life. He then pointed to his successor as the *bearer of goodness*, the teacher of morality, the teacher of righteousness, who had been incarnated as Jeshu ben Pandira, the teacher of the Essenes, about one hundred years before Christ. Rudolf Steiner identified Jeshu ben Pandira as an earlier incarnation of this bodhisattva who was known to the Essenes as the *teacher of righteousness*—the teacher of the good.[25] Further, from Rudolf Steiner's indications we can go back some four centuries prior to the incarnation as Jeshu ben Pandira (about 100 BC) to the incarnation of this same individuality as Kashyapa at the time of Gautama Buddha (sixth/fifth centuries BC).[26] And we can go back further still to the incarnation of this individuality as Abraham (second millennium BC), who was the founder of

---

24 For a deeper discussion, see Powell, *Cultivating Inner Radiance and the Body of Immortality*, chapter 5.

25 Steiner held two lectures about Jeshu ben Pandira in Leipzig, Nov. 4 and 5, 1911; for a summary see page 1 of the article by Powell, "Valentin Tomberg Symposium 2009 Report: Valentin Tomberg and the Bodhisattva of the 20th Century" (www.sophiafoundation.org/articles).

26 See my article "Kashyapa and the Proclamation of Christ in the Etheric," *Starlight*, vol. 11, no. 1 (Easter 2011); free download from the Sophia Foundation website (www.sophiafoundation.org/activities/newsletter).

the chosen people, the people of Israel, the people who were to prepare for the coming of Christ in a physical body.[27] Abraham-Kashyapa-Jeshu ben Pandira, who will be the future Maitreya Buddha, the Bearer of the Good, is destined to be the transmitter of the impulse of Christ in his Second Coming and on into the far-distant future. Christ *is* the Good, and the Bearer of the Good is, in a certain respect, a Christ-Bearer.

❀

THE APOCALYPTIC BATTLE

Given the significance of this time since the year 2000—the new "Abraham epoch" spoken of by Rudolf Steiner (see foreword)—and given the background of the incarnation as Abraham, the founder of Ancient Israel, as another indication for the identity of this successor to Rudolf Steiner, it is evident that it is a matter of someone who undoubtedly bears inwardly a panoramic overview of the Old Testament, a perspective that comprises the history of Ancient Israel. Moreover, as the bearer of the principle and impulse of goodness, this bodhisattva is clearly intimately connected with

---

27 In his lecture in Karlsruhe, on Jan. 25, 1910, Steiner implicitly identifies Abraham as the individuality whose mission it will be to prepare humanity for the vision of Christ in his etheric body, when he says, in the context of Christ's Second Coming, "It will be known that, just as Abraham preceded Christ as a preparer, he also takes over the mission, after Christ's coming, of being a helper in his work" (Steiner, *The True Nature of the Second Coming*, p. 19). This is just one of many statements made by Rudolf Steiner about Abraham as the individuality who will be the *actual proclaimer* of Christ's coming in the etheric realm—in other words, the Jeshu ben Pandira individuality. A more recent translation of this passage reads: "We will realize that, even as Abraham preceded Christ and prepared his way, Abraham also assumed the task of helping later on with the work of Christ" (Steiner, *The Reappearance of Christ in the Etheric*, p. 21); and, p. 21: "The one who led humanity's descent into the physical plane will reappear after Christ and lead humanity upward to reunite with the spirit worlds." From the context, it appears that "the one" whom Steiner is speaking of here is Abraham.

Christ, having a profound relationship with everything that is expressed in the New Testament and in the Book of Revelation. When we contemplate the deep connection of this reincarnated Abraham-Kashyapa-Jeshu ben Pandira individuality with the mysteries of the Bible, we see a relationship between Rudolf Steiner and his successor as expressed in the relationship between truth and goodness.

With the Maitreya individuality, the primary focus is on the Good. We can think of this as expressing something of the difference in orientation between Gautama Buddha and the Maitreya Buddha. Gautama Buddha brought the impulse of focusing on helping individuals to become better human beings through the eightfold path, through developing virtue, especially compassion. Here a difference with the Maitreya Buddha is revealed, particularly when we consider the image associated with him—or, rather, with the Kalki Avatar—riding on a white horse, with a two-edged sword issuing from his mouth. What are the two edges of his sword? One is for the good, and the other is for the fight against evil. This belongs to the impulse of the Maitreya Buddha/Kalki Avatar individuality, whose mission takes account of the fact that in the post-Christian era there is a fight, a great battle between good and evil—this being the theme of the Apocalypse.

Since we are free beings, we do not *have* to take part in this battle unless called to do so. It is very important to know that taking up the battle with evil is a *calling* and, in fact, it would be foolhardy for someone to try to undertake anything in the battle with evil unless that person felt a definite calling to do so. In this connection there are some inspiring words of Valentin Tomberg (1900–1973) from his *Studies on the Apocalypse*, where he draws our attention to what this battle is about. He talks about the forces that are working against the true Christ impulse in the world, indicating that even in nominally Christian countries to a certain extent Christianity has been done away with in business, politics, and the realm of science. It is a matter of "the banishment of Christianity from all areas of life." In referring to Christianity, he is speaking here of *true Christianity arising from the Christ impulse.*

> The banishment of Christianity from all areas of life goes on and on, and the realities of the physical world arrange themselves in stronger and stronger opposition to Christianity and in opposition to the love-filled light of wisdom which is just as essential to the human soul as are sunlight and warmth to a plant.[28]

Here he is saying that Christ and Sophia, love and wisdom, are as essential to the human soul as sunlight and warmth to the plant, and that we see in the world more and more how this possibility is excluded.

> From this view of Christianity, the human world is empty and cold. Indeed the realities of the physical world of humanity are gradually developing in a way that Christianity has been reduced. What Christian truth can manifest in present-day life—that is, without having to protect itself everywhere through compromise? Only in the *word* can the Christ impulse become a reality among the people of today. This is important because it is the essential impulse of the Maitreya, who, as the Bearer of the Good, is destined to bring to manifestation the power of the word as a force for the Good.
>
> True Christianity today has the same opportunity as does the word to live in the world without becoming adulterated and falsified by compromise; it is a time of great testing. The vast and powerful realities of today's "Chastel Merveille" [the expression for the anti-Grail castle, the castle of Klingsor, which is active in the world at this time] are opposed only by the word and nothing else at all. The millions of Christians cannot and must not be arrayed to do battle with the organized anti-Christian millions. Anti-Christian forces cannot and must not be fought with the

---

28 Tomberg, *Christ and Sophia*, p. 343.

use of their own weapons. Power, number, and organization—all are opposed only by the word borne by the human voice. The test is this: Despite everything, we must never say, "These are mere words; they are not the realities." Rather, because they can be only words, the *whole* reality of the Christ impulse must be experienced *in* them.[29]

In his "Studies of the Apocalypse," just quoted, Tomberg has much more to say about this (referred to in the Book of Revelation), where he points out that there is a "little strength" against the "colossal power" which is arrayed against the Good. This "little strength" is referred to in these words of Christ:

> I know your deeds. See, I have placed before you an open door that no one can shut. I know that you have little strength, yet you have kept my word and have not denied my name. (Rev. 3:8)

Here it is clearly indicated that we have to side with the *little strength* against the great strength of untruth and evil in the world—i.e., we have to align ourselves with the power of the word. And, moreover, we must refrain from denying the name of Christ. This means on the one hand that we are called upon to uphold the true ideals of the Christ impulse in spite of the great power of external realities that are currently arrayed against them. And on the other hand the appeal made here is not to deny the name of Christ, since this would essentially be tantamount to excluding the power of the Good itself—as Christ *is* the Good.

> The faculty of the *word* and that of *moral logic* (keeping the word and not denying the name) will be most highly developed at the beginning of the sixth epoch, that of Philadelphia [Rev. 3:7], when the Maitreya Buddha, the "Bringer of Goodness," will appear. The special task of the Maitreya is to develop what has "little strength"—the *word* and the *thought*—into a power that will regain a position in the world

---

29 Ibid.

that allows a cultural community to evolve. The moral force of the word will live and work so powerfully in the Maitreya that human beings will be stopped and will experience a spiritual conversion...through the magical, moral influence of the word. Thoughts will no longer merely explain the nature of goodness, but actually transmit it. The Maitreya Buddha will not merely show goodness; he will awaken it in the soul.[30]

Through an astronomical understanding of the prophecy made in the *S'rîmad Bhâgavatam* referred to above, it would appear that the year 2014 could signify the time of emergence of the Kalki Avatar/Maitreya Buddha individuality in a new incarnation—his twenty-first-century incarnation. Bearing in mind Steiner's indication that this individuality incarnates in almost every century, this sequence of incarnations leads to the culminating incarnation in about two thousand five hundred years time when he will attain buddhahood and will then no longer incarnate on the Earth, but will continue to work from spiritual realms for the good of humanity and the Earth's evolution.

In the words of Steiner quoted earlier, "We are living today at the beginning of a period of transition before the onset of the next six-hundred-year wave of culture, when something *entirely new* is pressing in upon us, when the Christ impulse is to be enriched by something new."[31] What is meant here by *something entirely new*? In the same lecture, Steiner elucidates that it is the stream of Buddhism in a new form, enlivened by the Christ impulse, that is the "something new." And given that Kashyapa, the future Maitreya Buddha, is the successor of Gautama Buddha, it is abundantly clear that it is the Abraham-Kashyapa-Jeshu ben Pandira-Maitreya Buddha/Kalki Avatar individuality—the "bringer of the Good"—who is the one to spearhead the stream of Buddhism in a new form, enlivened by the Christ impulse. Thus

---

30 Ibid., p. 345.

31 Steiner, *Background to the Gospel of St. Mark*, p. 153.

we see how the prophecy of Steiner relating to the year 2014 emerges in a remarkable way in light of the ancient prophecy made in the *S'rîmad Bhâgavatam.*

For purposes of astrosophical study I am including the horoscope (see page 11) of the possible date of emergence of the Kalki Avatar on July 27, 2014, where it can be seen that the New Moon (conjunction of Sun and Moon at 9° Cancer) is in conjunction with Jupiter (7½° Cancer)—all in the *nakshatra Pushya,* which extends from 4° Cancer to 17° Cancer (see horoscope and see also the entry for July 27 in the commentaries in the 2014 issue of the *Journal for Star Wisdom*).[32] It is also interesting, according to this horoscope, that at this time the position of Pluto in Sagittarius is transiting the position of the Sun in Sagittarius at the birth of Jesus of Nazareth, whose birth is described in the Gospel of Luke, and that Pluto is close to where it was located at the historical events of Christ's Ascension and Pentecost. Moreover, in this horoscope Saturn is located at its place of exaltation in the zodiac, in conjunction with the brightest star, the alpha star, in Libra. The conjunction of Saturn with this star[33]—referred to as Saturn's *exaltation*—was seen as the most powerful location of Saturn in the entire zodiac:

> In the case of the exaltation of Saturn at 21° Libra, the Babylonians saw that Saturn was exalted when it appeared in conjunction with the star Zubenelgenubi, the brightest star in Libra, marking the southwestern end of the beam of the

---

32 Powell, ed., *Journal for Star Wisdom 2014,* with articles by various authors, heliocentric and geocentric ephemerides, and commentaries by Claudia McLaren Lainson regarding the more significant planetary configurations.

33 Powell and Bowden, *Astrogeographia,* p. 37, gives the exact location of the alpha star of Libra, Zubenelgenubi, as 20°17' Libra; see the table of exaltations of the planets on page 37. For the Babylonians each planet has a particular location in the zodiac, usually designated by its conjunction with a particular star or star cluster, where is it most powerful. This location where a planet is most powerful in the zodiac is referred to as the planet's *exaltation.*

Balance. The exact degree of this star is 20½° Libra, so the exaltation should be corrected from 21° to 20½° Libra. In this case the original specification of the exaltation of Saturn—the star Zubenelgenubi—was (after the introduction of the zodiac) equated with the zodiacal longitude of 21° Libra.[34]

Given the long-standing association of Saturn with righteousness, taken together with the Scales of Libra denoting the symbol of the law in the legal profession, that this position was seen as Saturn's exaltation is understandable. In this connection it is interesting to consider that the Maitreya individuality, in his incarnation as Jeshu ben Pandira, the teacher of the Essenes, was referred to as the *teacher of righteousness*. It is this quality of righteousness that is lacking at this time of the reign of the Antichrist, who is referred to by St. Paul as the *man of lawlessness.*

Concerning the coming of our Lord Jesus Christ and our being gathered to him.... Don't let anyone deceive you in any way, for that day will not come until the rebellion occurs and the man of lawlessness is revealed, the man doomed to destruction. He will oppose and will exalt himself over everything that is called God or is worshiped, so that he sets himself up in God's temple, proclaiming himself to be God....

The secret power of lawlessness is already at work; but the one who now holds it back will continue to do so until he is taken out of the way. And then the lawless one will be revealed, whom the Lord Jesus will overthrow with the breath of his mouth and destroy by the splendor of his coming. The coming of the lawless one will be in accordance with how Satan works. He will use all sorts of displays of power through signs and wonders that serve the lie, and all the ways that wickedness deceives those who are perishing. They perish because they refused to love the truth and so be saved. For this reason God sends them a powerful delusion so that they will believe the lie and so that all will be condemned who have not believed the truth but have delighted in wickedness.

---

34   Ibid., p. 34.

But we ought always to thank God for you, brothers and sisters loved by the Lord, because from the beginning God chose you to be saved through the sanctifying work of the Spirit and through belief in the truth. He called you to this through our gospel, that you might share in the glory of our Lord Jesus Christ.

So then, brothers and sisters, stand firm and hold fast to the teachings we passed on to you, whether by word of mouth or by letter. May our Lord Jesus Christ himself and God our Father, who loved us and by his grace gave us eternal encouragement and good hope, encourage your hearts and strengthen you in every good deed and word. (2 Thes. 2:1–17)

A man of righteousness—according to the research presented here: the Abraham-Kashyapa-Jeshu ben Pandira-Maitreya Buddha/ Kalki Avatar individuality—is prophesied to arise at this time of the reign of the man of lawlessness. The contrast of righteousness and iniquity is spoken of by Christ in Matthew 13 in connection with his Second Coming, his return as the Son of Man in great power and glory accompanied by angels:

The Son of Man will send out his angels, and they will weed out of his kingdom everything that causes sin and all who do evil. They will throw them into the blazing furnace, where there will be weeping and gnashing of teeth. Then the righteous will shine like the sun in the kingdom of their Father. Whoever has ears, let them hear. (Matt. 13:41–43)

If the research presented in this article is accurate, the time referred to by St. Paul, when Christ will overthrow the Antichrist "with the breath of his mouth and destroy by the splendor of his coming" will be shortly after the winter solstice of 2016, at the end of the 3½-year reign of the prince of darkness. In the words of the Russian poet and seer, Daniel Andreev:

The prince of darkness will terrify human beings.... Christ, however, will take on as many forms as there are consciousnesses on Earth to behold him. He will adapt himself to everyone, and will converse with all. His forms, in an unimaginable way, will simultaneously yield an image: *One who appears in heaven surrounded by unspeakable glory.* There will not be a single being on Earth who will not see the Son of God and hear his Word.[35]

THE 3½ YEARS

Intensive engagement with and study of the most incisive esoteric problems of our time is still largely suppressed and avoided in today's anthroposophic movement. Likewise the equally significant and striking utterances by Steiner about the mystery of the reappearance of the etheric Christ and the impulse of his adversary, the Antichrist, in the twentieth and twenty-first centuries, are only seldom examined, illumined or cited, although the drastic nature of these comments, along with the radical form in which they were expressed, ought to place every student of anthroposophy on the highest alert. In perception of and engagement with this highly topical phenomenon of our times, a scarcely explicable kind of paralysis seems to have taken hold of human spirits. There seems no other way to explain this paralysis than as the latent effect of the power of the Antichrist himself.

If one begins to speak of this theme, even very tentatively, the reactions one receives—from anxiety through to fairly inexplicable, outright rejection—show how people unconsciously experience and perceive this power as very present and real.

If the student of anthroposophy wishes to regard himself as a true pupil of anthroposophy, his first task is to devote himself entirely to the Christ Mystery with all his thinking, feeling, and will. This Christ Mystery, however, inevitably encompasses the Mystery of his adversary. The esoteric pupil could not learn to grasp the deeds of Christ—both those at the turning point of time and those of the contemporary

---

35   Quoted from Powell, *Prophecy–Phenomena–Hope*, p. 89.

Christ being today—and could never develop a fuller under-standing of the Christ being and his significance for future human evolution let alone find the path to redemption, if he did not also enquire into all that seeks to prevent him from following his Redeemer.

The esoteric laws show, though, that it is not up to the lower human will whether the initiation pupil does or does not wish to concern himself with a particular theme on the path of initiation. Whosoever desires to become an esoteric pupil in the anthroposophic…sense, will only be able to pursue a single path: that of the Representative of Humanity. And he will therefore encounter everything that the Representative of Humanity encountered and still encounters.[36]

I begin this section with this quotation from Judith von Halle because it expresses a profound truth: Christ—the Representative of Humanity—must be at the center of our thoughts, heart, and consciousness, if we turn our attention to consider the influences of evil. On this account, it may be that some readers might prefer to omit this section concerning the 3½ years and leave it for later. And for others the question may arise: Why look at the struggle between good and evil at all?

Because the Maitreya is the bearer of the good, the confrontation between good and evil is clearly relevant to our theme. Here we touch upon a deep mystery relating to the activity of Christ in our time, in the etheric realm, bearing in mind that the Maitreya–Kalki individuality is a primary representative of Christ at this time. On the one hand Christ, with his Second Coming, is sacrificing himself anew, this time on the etheric level, for the sake of the spiritualization of Mother Earth—for the creation, ultimately, of the "New Earth" (Rev. 21:1). And on the other hand Christ is leading the higher self or *spirit self* of the human being into relationship with the human "I." The higher

---

36   Von Halle, *Descent into the Depths of the Earth on the Anthroposophic Path of Schooling*, pp. 49–50.

self beholds in spiritual realms—so to say as the "upper eye"—and the "I" as the "lower eye" perceives what is taking place in the outer world, which, especially at this time of the Antichrist, is becoming increasingly an expression of evil. By means of the "upper eye" we may know the intentions of the good, and through the "lower eye" those of evil.

Seeing with both eyes simultaneously is the ultimate goal, signifying the attainment of true wisdom in its fullness. At this time of the Second Coming, the human being's task is to see with the "upper eye" and the "lower eye" simultaneously—this being the prerequisite for true freedom, in the spirit of Christ's words: "You will know the truth, and the truth will set you free" (John 8:32). "This simultaneous sight through the upper and lower 'eyes' is possible only when a relationship exists between them, and the bond between knowing goodness and knowing evil is the Christ impulse in the human 'I'."[37] In chapters two to seven, contributed by Estelle Isaacson, the main focus is upon the realm of goodness as beheld by way of the "upper eye"; and in this section on the 3½ years it is a matter of seeing with the "lower eye" what is taking place in the world at the present time. Seeing with both "eyes" is possible through the Christ impulse in the human "I."

Regarding the 3½ years referred to above: the 3½ years of the rule of the Antichrist is a theme that has been addressed in my book *Prophecy-Phenomena-Hope: The Real Meaning of 2012* and in the book, written together with Kevin Dann, *Christ & the Maya Calendar: 2012 and the Coming of the Antichrist*. As I have shown scientifically in an earlier book, *Chronicle of the Living Christ*, the length of Christ's ministry from the baptism to the resurrection was 3½ years or 1290 days (this is actually twelve days longer than the exact period of 3½ years amounting to 1278 days). A period of three years and six months is mentioned in

---

37 Tomberg, *Christ and Sophia*, pp. 383–385, offers a profound exposition concerning the working together of the "upper eye" and the "lower eye."

Luke 4:25, which, as discussed in *Chronicle of the Living Christ*, can be interpreted in relation to the 3½ years of Christ's ministry. On the other hand, two periods of approximately 3½ years are referred to in Daniel 12:11–12—an initial period of 1290 days and a subsequent period of 1,335 days. As described in *Prophecy-Phenomena-Hope* (pp. 59–65), this evidently refers to the preparatory 3½ years and the culminating 3½ years of the Antichrist's rule, which is characterized in these words: "The beast was given a mouth to utter proud words and blasphemies and to exercise its authority for forty-two months" (Rev. 13:5).[38]

In the "end times" discourse of Jesus to the disciples in the Gospel of Matthew, the same expression—the "abomination of desolation"—is referred to (Matt. 24:15) as in Daniel 12:11. This is a clear reference to the presence of the Antichrist—in particular, to the desolation wrought by what Vladimir Solovyov calls the "Antichrist's army."[39] A modern-day scenario of the significance of these words of the Prophet Daniel for our time emerges in considering the invasion of one country after another by the "world army" of the Antichrist, leaving behind untold death, misery, and desolation—the "abomination of desolation"—in the wake of each invasion.[40]

---

38   Why has a 3½-year period been granted to the Antichrist, the incarnated Ahriman? This obviously has to do with the fact of the 3½ years of Christ's ministry, in that the Antichrist is being granted the same period of time in his attempt to win over—away from Christ—all human beings to his side. For an understanding concerning the long-standing conflict between Christ and Ahriman, see Powell and Dann, *Christ and the Maya Calendar*.

39   "A Short Tale of the Antichrist," in Solovyov, *War, Progress, and the End of History*.

40   For a graphic depiction of what the "abomination of desolation" looks like, see the 19-minute video (at http://www.informationclearinghouse. info/article33166.htm), revealing one aspect of the world as it is taking shape with the use of high-tech weapons against defenseless civilians, whereby Ahriman feeds on the immense suffering that innocent men, women, and children are undergoing. His goal is to maximize human suffering. The "abomination of desolation" amounts to the creation of "Hell on Earth."

For those readers unfamiliar with the background depicted in my aforementioned books, the term "Antichrist" in the Christian tradition, *and as it is used here in this book*, is the same as what Rudolf Steiner refers to as the *incarnation of Ahriman*. From Rudolf Steiner's indications, a parallel can be drawn between the incarnation of Christ in Jesus, which lasted for 1,290 days, and the incarnation of Ahriman in a human being (Mr. X), lasting for 3½ years. This is a vast and complex theme, which cannot be discussed here in any detail. However, the quotes from Daniel Andreev's article "Rose of the World" in the *Journal for Star Wisdom*[41] give some helpful indications—helpful for our understanding of the present time of the Antichrist's activity in the world—including the indication that in his previous incarnation Mr. X was Joseph Stalin (1878–1953). It is this indication, combined with spiritual research—through which I was able to follow the soul of Stalin into his current incarnation as the vessel for Ahriman—that made it possible to determine the date for the onset of the period of the lawless one's rule. Based on this research the 3½ years possibly commenced around June 19, 2013. See the horoscope (next page) comparing the planetary configuration on this date with the birth horoscope of Stalin.

It can be seen from this horoscope comparison that the conjunction of the Sun and Jupiter on June 19, 2013, is opposite the conjunction of the Sun and Venus at the birth of Stalin—and, moreover, that the Sun at Stalin's birth was in conjunction with the galactic center (2° Sagittarius). Although, with little or no justification, most modern astronomers think of the galactic center as a *supermassive black hole*, this great center is called by Daniel Andreev, on the basis of a mystical vision he had of the galactic center, the *creative heart of our universe*.[42] On June 19, 2013, the

---

41   *Journal for Star Wisdom 2014*, p. 15.

42   Andreev, *The Rose of the World*, p. 198; see also, Powell and Dann, *Christ and the Maya Calendar*, appendix 1, "The Central Sun."

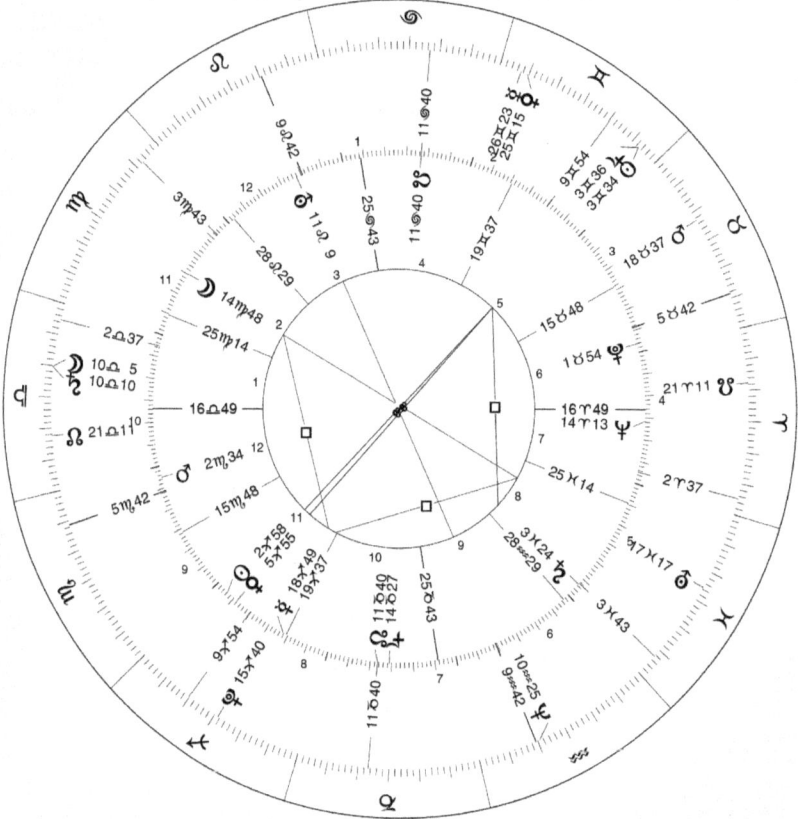

Comparison Chart

Outer - Geocentric
Event of Incarnation of Ahriman 1
At Washington, District of Columbia, Dist o, Latitude 38N53', Longitude 77W2'
Date: Wednesday, 19/JUN/2013, Gregorian
Time: 11:10, Time Zone EDT
Sidereal Time 3:53:52, Vernal Point 5 ♓ 4'20"

Inner - Geocentric
Birth of Joseph Stalin (V. !)
At Gori/Tiflis/Georgia, Latitude 42N00', Longitude 44E05'
Date: Wednesday, 6/DEC/1878, Julian
Time: 3:39, Local Time
Sidereal Time 9:24:50, Vernal Point 6 ♓ 56'58"

House System: Placidus, Zodiac: Sidereal SVP
Aspect set: Conjunction/Square/Opposition

galactic center was opposed by the conjunction of the Sun and Jupiter. Normally, of course, this configuration would not indicate something gravely negative.

How can one identify Mr. X on the world stage? "Ahriman promotes the illusion, the lie.... Ahriman lives upon lies; he is a spirit of untruth, the father of lies."[43] Much of what was put

_____

43   See http://www.bibliotecapleyades.net/biblianazar/ahrimano1.htm; Robert S. Mason's website "The Advent of Ahriman."

forward by Stalin was a lie, including his official date of birth. So it is with Mr. X: his date and place of birth—indeed, much of his "official biography"—are nothing but a web of lies. The lie—and, correspondingly, deception—is one indicator of this individual. Another is Ahriman's quest for power, whereby his goal is to guide his protégé, Mr. X, to the highest seat of power—in order to rule the world as a kind of "world emperor."[44]

Yet another indicator: Whereas the incarnated Christ laid down his life for humanity and the Earth, the incarnated Ahriman seeks to rule the world by abrogating to himself the right to be able to kill anyone on the Earth or to imprison anyone indefinitely, as Stalin did when he sent millions of Russians to the Soviet forced labor camp system known as the Gulag. And just as one of Stalin's primary focuses was the "kill list," which identified those he and others (of his close advisors) wanted to be killed, it can also be expected—as a karmic signature—that the Antichrist will also oversee a secret kill list in our time.[45]

Yet another indicator: This has to do with his *world army*, which wreaks death and destruction—the *abomination of desolation*—wherever it goes.[46] Thus, through the use of destructive

---

44 Anonymous, *Meditations on the Tarot*, chapter 4, has much to say about the "post" of emperor—that, for example, it was the striving of Napoleon, and then, later, Hitler, to seize the post of emperor in their quest for ultimate power: to rule over the whole world.

45 Stalin is held responsible for the death of millions of Russians and Ukrainians. "The consensus figure for those that Joseph Stalin murdered when he ruled the Soviet Union is 20,000,000.... The figure comes from the book by Robert Conquest, *The Great Terror: Stalin's Purge of the Thirties* (Macmillan 1968).... As for Stalin, when the holes in Conquest's estimates are filled in, I calculate that Stalin murdered about 43,000,000 citizens and foreigners, over twice Conquest's total. Therefore, the usual estimate of 20 million killed in Soviet democide is far off for the Soviet Union per se, and even less than half of the total Stalin alone murdered" (R. J. Rummel, Professor Emeritus at the University of Hawaii; http://www.distributedrepublic.net/archives/2006/05/01/how-many-did-stalin-really-murder).

46 In *Dirty Wars: The World is a Battlefield*, Jeremy Scahill, author of the *New York Times* bestseller *Blackwater*, takes us inside America's new

military actions a "hell on earth" is engineered. An example of this is the aftermath of cruise missile assaults, in which targeted regions are transformed into wastelands of death. Such is the preferred method of attack by the Antichrist through his world army. This destruction is vastly accelerated and amplified by the use of "uranium depleted" material in the bombs that desolate the earthly realm with radioactivity, ensuring a deathly and deadly impact for billions of years.[47] The onomatopoeic structure of the sequence

---

covert wars. The foot soldiers in these battles operate globally and inside the United States with orders from the White House to do whatever is necessary to hunt down, capture or kill individuals designated by the president as enemies.

Drawn from the ranks of the Navy SEALs, Delta Force, former Blackwater and other private security contractors, the CIA's Special Activities Division and the Joint Special Operations Command (JSOC), these elite soldiers operate worldwide, with thousands of secret commandos working in more than one hundred countries. Funded through "black budgets," Special Operations Forces conduct missions in denied areas, engage in targeted killings, snatch and grab individuals and direct drone, AC-130 and cruise missile strikes. While the Bush administration deployed these ghost militias, President Barack Obama has expanded their operations and given them new scope and legitimacy.

Dirty Wars follows the consequences of the declaration that "the world is a battlefield," as Scahill uncovers the most important foreign policy story of our time. From Afghanistan to Yemen, Somalia and beyond, Scahill reports from the front lines in this high-stakes investigation and explores the depths of America's global killing machine. He goes beneath the surface of these covert wars, conducted in the shadows, outside the range of the press, without effective congressional oversight or public debate. And, based on unprecedented access, Scahill tells the chilling story of an American citizen marked for assassination by his own government.

As US leaders draw the country deeper into conflicts across the globe, setting the world stage for enormous destabilization and blowback, Americans are not only at greater risk—we are changing as a nation. Scahill unmasks the shadow warriors who prosecute these secret wars and puts a human face on the casualties of unaccountable violence that is now official policy: victims of night raids, secret prisons, cruise missile attacks and drone strikes, and whole classes of people branded as "suspected militants." Through his brave reporting, Scahill exposes the true nature of the dirty wars the United States government struggles to keep hidden. See also the film Dirty Wars—http://dirtywars.org/the-film.

47   See http://www.nuclearreader.info/chapter6.html; "All weapons that contain DU ['depleted uranium'] are considered to be radioactive poison

of sounds "abomination of desolation" (an expression translated from the Hebrew and Greek original texts of the Bible[48]) is interesting, for bombs and their resultant desolations are an abomination against the Earth and humanity.

Moreover, whereas Christ is the protector and nurturer of life on Earth, Ahriman seeks to replace divine creation with his own creation: artificial or virtual reality on the level of human consciousness, and genetically manipulated organisms on the level of the plant and animal kingdoms. It can be expected that the Antichrist—the incarnated Ahriman—will exercise all his coercive power in occupying the position of "the most powerful man on the Earth," using financial means, trickery and manipulation, and even the threat of the immense military power at his disposal, to enforce the "blessing" of genetically modified seeds upon all humankind, unless this deadly threat to life on Earth is actively resisted by a sufficient number of morally awakened human beings who are more concerned with the future of life on this planet than with submitting to the deathly, profit-motivated agenda of the giant agribusiness corporations. These diabolical, ruthless business entities are obsessed with the lure of unspeakable power over all humanity and are driven by greed for the immense profits that will flow into their coffers as a result of their increasing control

---

gas weapons and as such they violate the Geneva Conventions under the 1925 Geneva Poison Gas Control Protocol. DU weapons are a permanent terrain contaminant and have a half-life of 4.5 billion years. DU can cause DNA damage, as well as cancer, leukemia and tragic birth defects. It is a kidney, liver, and neurotoxin. Multiple independent studies confirm this. There is a list of references documenting DU health damage on Wikipedia. DU has been blamed for the effects of Gulf War Syndrome—typified by chronic pain, extreme fatigue and an array of diseases. Some studies of Gulf War veterans who had normal babies before the war found that 67% of babies born after the war have severe birth defects, including missing brains, eyes, organs, legs and arms, and blood diseases"; see also http://www.washingtonsblog.com/2013/08/the-u-s-and-israel-have-used-chemical-weapons-within-the-last-8-years.html.

48 The abomination of desolation is referred to three times in the Book of Daniel (9:27, 11:31, 12:11) and in Matt. 24:15–16 and Mark 13:14.

of the entire world's food production. Their goal, toward which the Antichrist is helping them, is the total control of all food consumed by human beings.[49] Here it is a clear choice between Life and Death—between on the one hand the life stemming from the divine spark inherent in all of God's creation and indwelling the whole of Nature, and on the other hand the death inherent in genetically modified seeds. Especially virulent are those seeds into which "killer cells" have been implanted, which can only bring forth death-bringing "virtual plants" that when consumed inevitably lead to illness: tumors, malformation, sterility and, ultimately, death.[50] These plants may appear outwardly to be the same as real plants. However, having been removed from the cycle of life, and

---

49   There is a deep esoteric background to the GMO challenge for humanity at the present time, and this has to do with the fact, revealed by the Apocalypse code described in *Christ and the Maya Calendar*, that humanity as a whole is now undergoing the third temptation in the wilderness, that of "turning stones into bread"—this being the "purely Ahrimanic" temptation. This is the "virtual reality" temptation, made possible through technology, of making what is dead ("stones") appear to be living ("bread"). This is exactly the case with plants stemming from genetically manipulated organisms. These plants appear to be living, but the divine spark has been driven out from them and they are, from the perspective of the all-embracing etheric realm of the biosphere, actually dead.

50   See http://rt.com/news/monsanto-rats-tumor-france-531/; "French scientists have revealed that rats fed on GMO corn sold by American firm Monsanto, suffered tumors and other complications including kidney and liver damage"; also http://www.naturalnews.com/036710 _GMO_animal_experiments_infertility.html; "A study presented at the Days of Defense Against Environmental Hazards in Russia has unveiled once again the implicit dangers associated with the consumption of genetically-modified organisms (GMOs). According to Voice of Russia, scientists from the National Association for Gene Security and the Institute of Ecological and Evolutional Problems discovered that animals fed GMOs as part of their normal diet eventually develop the inability to reproduce.... Using hamsters as the test subjects, scientists observed that consumption of GM soybeans, which have never been a part of these creatures' normal diets, tended to slow sexual maturity and gradually eliminate the ability to reproduce. After several generations, hamsters consuming the 'Frankensoy' eventually lost their innate ability to reproduce."

thereby having lost the divine spark, they are a kind of "virtual reality" in the divine kingdom of Nature.

And still another indicator: the mission of humanity—in and through Christ—is to bring to realization freedom and love. Freedom is a most precious gift. Christ leaves us free. In freedom we are able to come to love in the spirit of the three aspects of love taught by Christ:

1. Love the Lord your God with all your heart and with all your soul and with all your strength and with all your mind;
2. Love your neighbor as yourself (Luke 10:27); and
3. Love your enemies (Matt. 5:44).

In contrast, an indicator of the Antichrist—in the guise of "protecting" human beings—is to direct against humankind a regime embodying the opposite of freedom and love. In this regime of the Antichrist, instead of the freedom of each individual being respected, the goal is to establish a worldwide surveillance state. The regime of the Antichrist seeks to bring to realization the opposite of freedom by spying upon everyone, to the degree that this is technologically possible in our digital age, by gathering communications of human beings around the globe. One of the consequences of the global spying regime is to create an atmosphere of suspicion and mistrust, thus generating separation between peoples and individuals that effectively stifles the unfolding of love, which flourishes in an atmosphere of familial love.

The grossest example of such an encroachment on freedom was the Stasi of Russian controlled East Germany. Estimates cite that there were an astonishing 480,000 agents of the Stasi. "The Stasi officers knew no limits and had no shame when it came to 'protecting the party and the state.' Absolutely nothing was sacred to the secret police."[51] The revelations exposing the vast reach

---

51 Worldwide surveillance is made possible through modern technology and is far more sophisticated and all-encompassing than the "primitive" surveillance methods of the Gestapo, the KGB, and the Stasi. However,

of the American government's spying programs, not to mention detainments without due process, are emblematic of the demise of freedom. This loss of freedom is characteristic of Ahriman's morbid presence.

In relation to the above indications regarding the Antichrist, Daniel Andreev presciently wrote: "Only much later, when the [alleged] 'savior' holds the entire power in his hands, will he show his true force."[52]

From these indications, it is evident that the choice now confronting every human being on the planet at this time is: *Christ or Antichrist*. This choice means that either we submit to the prince of darkness or we choose to align ourselves with the living Christ, now manifesting in the etheric realm. Often at critical junctures in the evolution of humanity, such as the beginning of a new cultural wave, an existential choice of this nature needs to be made.

Moreover, it is a matter, above all, of *consciously* choosing the good in contrast to the evil. And there is an important dimension to bear in mind here, which is addressed by Rudolf Steiner in his "green demons" meditation.[53] The essence of this meditation is summarized by Erich and Margarete Kirchner-Bockholt: "The age of freedom is also characterized by the fact that human beings must learn to see through the attacks made by the demons, to entice their secrets from them and pass on to the [spiritual] hierarchies the knowledge thus gained."[54] In other words, it is a

---

the psychologically oppressive effect resulting from global surveillance will in the course of time be experienced in the same way—or perhaps will be even worse—than that of the Gestapo in Nazi Germany, the KGB in Soviet Union, and the Stasi in East Germany. Compare with http://www.nytimes.com/books/first/k/koehler-stasi.html.

52 Andreev, "Rose of the World" in *Journal for Star Wisdom 2014*, p. 15, (tr. R.P.).

53 See the end of this article, http://www.doyletics.com/arj/rudyitaw.htm; the "green demons" meditation given by Rudolf Steiner to Ita Wegman; in Kirchner-Bockholt, *Rudolf Steiner's Mission and Ita Wegman*, p. 131.

54 Ibid., p. 132.

specifically human task to "entice their secrets" from the demons, exposing them to the light of day, offering up the knowledge thus gained to the angelic hierarchies, who are thereby empowered to intervene on behalf of the Good. These words by no means do justice to the profound depths of the "green demons" meditation, but at least they convey something of this important task of exposing evil on the level of consciousness. In fact, as indicated by Valentin Tomberg, it is the "weapon of recognition" of evil that disempowers it, bearing in mind, as spoken of by Steiner, that Ahriman is the "embodiment of evil."[55]

> Ahriman cannot be overcome either by *combatting* the Ahrimanic element or by trying to convert it. The Ahrimanic influence can neither be coerced by force nor inwardly transformed. The point is to *recognize* the Ahrimanic element, not fear it. A courageous glance of recognition is the sword that limits Ahriman in the outer world; and the courage of self-knowledge is the force that renders the Ahrimanic nature powerless in the human subconscious. As for Ahriman, the point is not to grant him power over the soul, and that—with thanks to the weapon of recognition—all his attacks fail on account of uncompromising human courage. Stability and rocklike firmness are needed, not attacks or a desire to flee from Ahrimanic onslaughts. The Ahrimanic element is powerless if it cannot influence human beings with either fear or bribery. In such a condition of powerlessness, it receives no nourishment and disappears to a region where it can no longer exercise power. Ahriman will be defeated, because he will not be nourished. His power in the world looks enormous and overwhelming, but it is merely an *illusion* designed either to bribe or to frighten. Nonetheless, it is an *objective* illusion made up of *actual* external phenomena built upon illusions that immediately show themselves as such when confronted by courageous recognition and incorruptibility—that is, a refusal to compromise, since all compromise is the result of bribery. That has been shown as a fact of cosmic experience

---

55   Steiner, *The Incarnation of Ahriman: The Embodiment of Evil.*

in the spiritual event of the Mystery of Golgotha traditionally called Christ's "descent into hell." ... Jesus Christ's "descent into hell" was the act that overcame Ahriman—not through superiority of power (that was not the issue), but by unveiling the extent of Ahriman's true power to an alert and uncompromising consciousness.[56]

Here we see how important the "weapon of recognition" is. How does one wield this weapon? First it is essential to hold in consciousness that Christ overcame Ahriman through his "descent into hell." This is the ground upon which one can stand with "stability and rocklike firmness." Fearlessly, one endeavors to cognize evil in the world—the actual as well as the intended evil—trying to discern the Antichrist's plan, as far as possible, in all its details, and at the same time one seeks to bring to consciousness the corresponding power of goodness in the heavens above that is the essence of Christ's intention for humankind and the Earth. What one cognizes as evil in the world is based on lies, and an important aspect of wielding the "weapon of recognition" is to seek the truth that is the counterpart to these lies. Once one has found the truth—and there are different levels to this: from a first flicker of truth, to a comprehensive grasp of a complex situation—one allows the light of truth to ray out from one's mind, so that inwardly one becomes a beacon for the light of truth. This is a powerful force with which the angelic hierarchies can unite to assist human beings in the great struggle with evil—a force that serves to keep Ahriman/the Antichrist in bounds. Wielding the "weapon of recognition" could be described as a *knightly activity*.

However, many people do not have any inclination to take up the path of wielding the "weapon of recognition" of evil. And some might have the view that if one practices "seeing no evil, hearing no evil, and speaking no evil," then all will be well. The following words by Sergey Baranov are addressed by him to all

---

56 Tomberg, *Christ and Sophia*, pp. 297–298 (trans. revised by R.P.).

those who, rather than taking up the knightly activity of cogniz-ing and exposing evil, believe that wishing for peace and a better world through prayer and meditation will eventually suffice to rid the world of evil.[57]

> Do you really think your wish for peace and a better world will influence corrupt and evil people that much so they will wake up one day and will realize how wrongly they were living before? And even if that were so, how long are you willing to wait? How many more people have to die in ille-gal, fraudulent wars? How much more does our planet have to be poisoned and destroyed before your wishful thinking will become a reality? Don't you realize that your dreams of tomorrow are someone's nightmares today? Well, I have a dif-ferent approach. And it is quite simple.
>
> I strive for a better world, just as you do. But I believe that exposing the evil is the way to diminish it, since evil's blood is secrecy; and draining it with transparency, it disperses like fog under the sun. If more people would understand this and would get involved—each in their own way—in exposing the fraud, corruption, and evil...thus waking up more people, I believe the world would be in a better shape than it is today. I'm sure you realize that in order to break free from the tyr-anny of King George, the Founding Fathers had to do more than just sitting in a circle while meditating on their freedom. Oppression continues if the oppressed remain silent. You are not a lonely voice. There are many of us who are on the right side of history. Truth is an immense force which doesn't need to be defended, but rather revealed and shared with as many

---

57　The author of this chapter believes it is important that there are those who—choosing not to focus their attention upon evil—wish for peace and a better world through prayer and meditation: this being one of the traditional practices in the Christian tradition (practiced, for example, by many monks and nuns). The perspective represented here is that it is *also* important that there are those who act as "Grail knights" by exposing evil through the "weapon of conscious recognition," as implied by Steiner's "green demons" meditation and as indicated in the foregoing quote from Tomberg. This latter path takes courage. If "uncompromising human courage" cannot be mustered, it is better not to try and cognize evil, but instead to focus solely upon the good.

people as possible. And when global awakening reaches a critical mass, change will come...washing the evil away like a tsunami. Use truth as a weapon, aiming it at all that is wrong. Don't let your fear become a cage for your mind.[58]

In the words of Valentin Tomberg:

Goodness *gains* by being known, while evil loses by being recognized as such. This is the essential difference between good and evil: good gains by being recognized; evil loses when it is recognized.[59]

As a historical archetype pointing to the stark contrast between two different realities—that of the Good springing forth from Christ and that of the forces of evil under the sway of the influence of Ahriman—let us consider the giving of the Law on Mt. Sinai more than three thousand years ago. While Moses, representing the forces of the Age of Aries,[60] was receiving up on the summit of Mt. Sinai the content of the Law, his brother Aaron down below at the foot of Mt. Sinai was inciting the people of Israel to institute the worship of the golden calf, representing a throwback to the preceding Age of Taurus the Bull. Aaron as high priest had influenced the people of Israel to donate their gold jewelry, which was melted down and then fashioned into the golden calf. After

---

58 Sergey Baranov, "What would it take to bring about change?"; http://intellihub.com/2013/08/22/what-would-it-take-to-bring-about-change/16.

59 Tomberg, *Christ and Sophia*, p. 299.

60 Steiner, *Deeper Secrets of Human History in the Light of the Gospel of St. Matthew*, Nov. 9, 1909: "A ram or lamb is sacrificed in place of Isaac.... The two horns of the Ram symbolize the sacrifice of the two-petalled lotus flower." The Age of Aries began with this event, and an indication that Moses was the primary representative of the Age of Aries is found in Steiner's Cosmogony lectures from 1906: see Steiner, *Kosmogonie* (Collected Works [CW] 94; Dornach, Switzerland: Rudolf Steiner Verlag, 2001), June 7, 1906: "The lotus flower with two petals is found on the brow.... One sees a symbol thereof in the two horns found on the brow of Moses" (trsl. by R.P.); also, July 10, 1906: "On his [statue of] Moses, Michelangelo represented the two-petalled lotus flower as two horns." This statue can be seen in Rome in the church of San Pietro in Vincoli (St. Peter-in-Chains).

creating this idol, Aaron had the people of Israel dancing around the golden calf. This was the scene that faced Moses when he came down from the summit of Mt. Sinai bearing the two stone tablets upon which Divine Law was inscribed. Moses, who was a great spiritual master, understood immediately what was at work here. He grasped, too, what needed to be done in order to turn around and overcome the evil forces invoked in the construction and worship of the golden calf by Aaron.

> Just imagine your teacher and master as being Moses: You direct your questions to him, asking why you cannot accelerate your progress in spite of your strong yearning to enter the spiritual world. Then you remain silent and await the response.... In most cases the figure of the golden calf will appear beside the figure of Moses, through whom fire will break out from the earth, which will devour the calf. And then Moses gives the ashes, dissolved in water, to you—the meditant—to drink.[61]

In this description, the golden calf represents the forces of the collective double or shadow of the people of Israel. Moses knew that these forces had to be given back to the children of Israel and dealt with by each person individually, which is why he prescribed what Rudolf Steiner described above as drinking "the ashes dissolved in water." Human beings are called to take up their inner work in order to meet the colossal forces of the collective shadow that will be set against humanity by the Antichrist, just as these forces were set against the children of Israel at the same time as Moses was receiving a mighty revelation of God.[62]

---

61   Steiner, *Esoteric Lessons 1910–1912*, Mar. 22, 1912 (tr. revised by R.P.).

62   As referred to in appendix 1: Against this background we can understand the overriding significance of Moses for the people of Israel, in that—as a bodhisattva—he was the bearer of the Archangel Michael, who was the Folk Spirit of that people. It was Michael who guided Moses to the sacred magical deed of giving the ashes dissolved in water to the people to drink. Michael is the "Lesser Guardian of the Threshold" to the spiritual world—Christ being the Greater Guardian—and it is

Analogously, spiritually beholding the current world situation, we see Christ in the etheric realm permeating and embracing the Earth's biosphere, and the Antichrist on the physical plane leading the people of this planet on a "contemporary dance"—a path of war and destruction, on the one hand, and a bowing down to the "golden calf" of the stock market, on the other hand—these being just two of numerous examples of contemporary activities that serve to strengthen the forces of the double, the shadow nature of the human being.

Sacred magic such as that employed by Moses needs to be wisely used now to turn around and halt the triumphant march of the forces of evil in their drive to implement their plan to conquer and tyrannize humankind under the direction of the Antichrist. It is especially the youth who are vulnerable to the agenda of the Antichrist. They are subject to a massive assault that begins long before they have reached their maturity—the time when the "I" of the human being becomes operative around the age of twenty-one. It is at this time that the "I" enters the human being as the divine spark that guides the individual along the path of his or her intended destiny. This birth of the "I" is a prerequisite for the birth of Christ within—expressed in the words of St Paul: "Not I, but Christ in me." The present-day attack by the Antichrist has the aim of "dumbing down" the "I" of all people, the goal being to preclude thereby the birth of Christ within. And with this same goal in view, the attack is also vehemently directed toward stunt-ing the coming-to-birth of the "I" in young people, who are the hope for the future of humanity and the Earth.

Thus, nowadays it is almost impossible to get young people to change their diets—for example, to stop eating GMO food, to find better water, and to breathe fresh air. The result is that many

---

Michael who reveals to each person their double or shadow, which is the responsibility of each person to deal with. In other words, the image of Michael holding the dragon underfoot applies also on an individual level for each person with respect to mastering one's own double or shadow.

people's organisms are compromised by way of all sorts of bacteria and parasites, as well as from DNA damage through the effects of prolonged exposure to electromagnetic radiation—these being just a few of the consequences of the current assault of evil forces upon human beings at this time of the Antichrist. What possible solutions are there to the attacks that are happening now, especially in relation to the youth?[63]

While it is almost impossible to describe briefly the complexity of the current situation of humanity and the Earth,[64] the answer to this situation lies in awakening to Christ in the etheric realm, whose being is unfathomable mercy and pure goodness. One can become attuned to his presence, and in the course of time become filled with his divine love and goodness. One gradually discovers, then, that it is possible to send this love across the Earth, the goal being to become so full of divine love and goodness that one is able to pour it out into the world for the healing of human beings and Nature. It is a matter of accessing the power of Christ's divine love and goodness—the power of the Divine which originally created everything—as *healing for the world*. This is the strongest power in existence.

Moreover, it is a matter also of *witnessing* love in order to enhance the healing flow. To grasp this, let us consider the following words by the anonymous author of the book *Meditations on the Tarot*: "It is not a matter of seeing…with human eyes, but rather of seeing with the eyes—and in the light—of Mary-Sophia."[65] At his

---

63 Powell, *Cultivating Inner Radiance and the Body of Immortality* is written to offer practices that help one align with Christ in the etheric realm and to develop "inner radiance" serving as a protection in relation to the assault of evil forces continually bombarding us, such as electromagnetic radiation, etc.

64 See Powell and Dann, *Christ and the Maya Calendar;* and Powell, *Prophecy–Phenomena–Hope,* for a deeper exposition concerning the complex multi-layered apocalyptic battle currently underway for possession of humanity and the Earth.

65 Anonymous, *Meditations on the Tarot,* p. 547.

sacrifice on Golgotha, Divine Love flowed through Christ for the healing of the Earth and humanity. It was of supreme importance that this event was witnessed by some fifteen holy women gathered around the cross.[66] The holy women were there as witnesses on behalf of Sophia. It was their presence—bearing witness—that enabled the healing power of Christ's Divine Love to flow all the more abundantly. Similarly, it was of supreme significance that Mary Magdalene, as a leading representative of Sophia, was present in the garden of the Holy Sepulcher on Easter Sunday morning to witness the Risen One. Through her presence, something was set in motion to which she bears witness throughout all time.[67]

Now let us consider this in connection with the Maitreya–Kalki individuality as the bringer of goodness. Goodness is a natural consequence of love. The fruit of the flow of love set in motion by Christ through his sacrifice on Golgotha is goodness. It is this which the Maitreya–Kalki individuality—as the bearer of the good—is representing, as a leading Christ representative who returns again and again into incarnation upon the Earth. And in a way analogous to the holy women at the foot of the Cross or to Mary Magdalene in the garden of the Holy Sepulcher, we are called to be witnesses to the Maitreya's deeds of sacred magic,[68] in order to enhance the healing power of the divine word of Christ embodied by the Maitreya. Thus can Christ's love be ever more consciously present, manifesting the Good in the world—not only through the Maitreya, but also through all human beings aligned with Christ in the current apocalyptic struggle with the evil one.

---

66   Only one disciple, John, was at the foot of the Cross, as a witness on behalf of the circle of twelve. However, as described by Anne Catherine Emmerich, *Visions of the Life of Christ*, there were fifteen or sixteen holy women present.

67   Concerning what was set in motion as a flow of Divine Light, Love, and Life from the Risen One to Mary Magdalene—as an archetype for all human beings to aspire to—see Robert Powell, *Cultivating Inner Radiance and the Body of Immortality*, pp. 27–28.

68   Anonymous, *Meditations on the Tarot*, chapter 3.

We are invited—in the footsteps of the Maitreya–Kalki individuality—to be participants in deeds of goodness. And we are also invited—seeing with the eyes and in the light of Sophia—to be witnesses to others' deeds of goodness: those of Christ and his disciples in the past, those of the Maitreya and his disciples and others in the present, and looking to the future deeds of the Good. Bearing witness on behalf of Sophia, we enhance the power of the Good.

In my book *Cultivating Inner Radiance and the Body of Immortality* I have outlined a path of practice for connecting with Christ in the etheric realm. There is a meditation by Valentin Tomberg which forms the basis for one of the exercises in this book, and which I would like to include in this chapter. From 1933 onward Valentin Tomberg stood in inner connection with the Christ in the etheric realm, and at Easter 1941 he communicated these words, indicating the name of the Etheric Christ as *AMEN*:

> The AMEN bears the World Word within as the Kingdom,
> And in the miracles and stages of the Passion wields the
> Power,
> And as the Risen One is the Glory.
> The Kingdom, the Power, and the Glory are united in Christ
> Jesus,
> And their fulfillment is the AMEN.
> His head is the Kingdom, embracing all the stars in the
> heavens.
> His breath is the Power to continue the work of creation, a
> breathing, radiant cross of light against the background
> of the starry heavens.
> And his limbs are the Glory of spirit-permeated substance,
> like a rainbow in the foreground.
> And the unity of the rainbow, the radiant cross of light,
> and the starry heavens is the all-encircling circle of the
> AMEN.[69]

---

69   Powell, *Cultivating Inner Radiance and the Body of Immortality*,
      pp. 39–40.

"His breath is the Power"—and according to St. Paul, in the passage quoted earlier: "And then the lawless one will be revealed, whom the Lord Jesus will overthrow with the breath of his mouth and destroy by the splendor of his coming." This is the blessing referred to by the Old Testament prophet Daniel at the end of the trial of the second 3½-year period: "Blessed is he who waits, and comes to the one thousand three hundred and thirty-five days" (Daniel 12:12). From June 19, 2013, it is 1290 days to December 29, 2016, or 1335 days to February 12, 2017—1290 days and 1335 days being the two periods mentioned by Daniel. Star wisdom is focused upon the glory of the starry heavens, of which—as indicated in the foregoing meditation—the head of the Etheric Christ is a manifestation: "His head is the Kingdom, embracing all the stars in the heavens."

Moreover, in the words of Daniel Andreev:

> Christ…will take on as many forms as there are consciousnesses on Earth to behold him. He will adapt himself to everyone, and will converse with all. His forms, in an unimaginable way, will simultaneously yield an image: *One who appears in heaven surrounded by unspeakable glory.* There will not be a single being on Earth who will not see the Son of God and hear his Word.[70]

Andreev's vision is in accordance with the words of the Book of Revelation: "Look, he is coming with the clouds, and every eye will see him" (Rev. 1:7). And in Steiner's words:

> Understanding the Mystery of Golgotha is the only thing that enables us to experience the whole of nature morally. If one then gazes up at the clouds and sees the lightning flashing from them, one will then be able to behold Christ in his etheric form. With the "clouds," that is to say with the elements, he will appear in spirit form. This vision will one day appear to every person.[71]

---

70   Quoted from Powell, *Prophecy–Phenomena–Hope*, p. 89.

71   Steiner, *"Freemasonry" and Ritual Work*, p. 374.

❀

The following brief characterization of the unfolding of the 3½ years of the Antichrist, considered as a trial that humankind is now undergoing, includes several aspects:

The first year is a time of coming to experience the *dark night of the soul*, during which there is no reference point for an inner sense of knowing the reality of oneself other than Christ, who accompanies us through this trial. Without Christ, the dark night of the soul can be an experience of great fear and overwhelming loneliness. One has to become aware at this time that a great battle is being waged for one's soul—and for every soul—a battle that is being waged on a subtle level. Also, one has to become aware of snares being set by the adversary, the Antichrist, whose dark forces seek to desolate human beings. In this situation it is of supreme importance to *hold to Christ*. To do this one has to first win over one's soul completely from the dark forces. *One can only do this for oneself* and then, increasingly, *one finds new love within the depths of the soul*. Further, one can turn to one's Guardian Angel, who is able to show one where one has gone astray from the true path—the true path being that of love.

In the second of the three years a great feeling of emptiness arises within human beings. There is a sense that everything is too difficult to comprehend. This is accompanied by increasing self-doubt and a sense of oppression. This can lead to the feeling that one is losing one's will. This is the experience of the void of the abyss, for it is the abyss separating the sensory realm from that of the spiritual at which one now stands. In contrast to the awareness of the battle for the soul being waged during the first year, the second year is characterized by the sense of being abandoned to oneself in a morass of nothingness, seeming like hell, accompanied by a sense of powerlessness. In this state of consciousness it is important to be aware that *there is something* within the nothingness. Then one can become aware of a flicker of light, and that underlying the light is the power of Christ's love—responding to one's own love for Christ. "Those who love me will keep my word, and my Father will love them, and we will come to them and make our home with them" (John 14:23). Then one will gradually come to know that there is no end to love, that Christ's love is enduring, and that he loves every human soul. The essence of the trial of nothingness in the second year is to lead one to the love within which enables one to find one's way out of the void. Underlying this is the realization that the world was created by love and that by the power of love it will be redeemed. Through the great love of Christ's sacrifice, he knows every human soul, and it is his love that is the lifeline that can lead the soul back to him.

In the period of the third year of the great trial, through the *love born within* during the second year of the 3½ years of the Antichrist, inner darkness can gradually be overcome through the light of love. Nevertheless, dark beings still seek to hinder and discourage one, for they cannot abide the inner light within one's soul. In the midst of these new challenges, it is important to focus ever more upon Christ as the light, love, and life of the world. The challenge here is that it will seem as if Christ is gone. This is the challenge that historically the disciples underwent at Christ's Ascension when he disappeared before their eyes. It was necessary for them to go through this experience in order to come to Pentecost, when the disciples had the experience of the birth of Christ within and became transformed into apostles. Hitherto they had been disciples, learning from the Master. And now, through the birth of Christ within, they became apostles, empowered to go out into the world and to teach and heal in the name of Christ. Daniel Andreev's words quoted above, where he speaks of Christ appearing in heaven simultaneously to every human being on the planet, appearing in unspeakable glory, is the new Pentecost—what Rudolf Steiner referred to as the *World Pentecost*. This event denotes the end of the 3½ years of the Antichrist, because the Antichrist will be overthrown, cast down, by the World Pentecost manifestation of Christ in unspeakable glory in the heavens. This will be accompanied by a beholding of a rainbow of colors emanating from Christ as he gradually draws closer and closer, bestowing upon human beings a sense of peace and unfathomable love. For Christ is unfathomable mercy, who calls all human beings to return to him—to return to love.[72]

❀

It is a privilege for me to write at the end of this chapter, by way of introduction to Estelle Isaacson's profound visions of the Kalki–Maitreya individuality in the following chapters, that I consider her two-volume work, *Through the Eyes of Mary Magdalene*, to be great inspirational works.[73] Volume 2, which focuses upon Christ's Passion, culminating with the Resurrection,[74] is particularly inspiring. While I cannot warrant her visions as being accurate in every detail, I have through years of personal acquaintance with Estelle and her visions gained ever more confidence in their overall accuracy, appropriateness, and moral depth. Her visions are, I believe, as elucidated in detail in the closing section of appendix I, an example of the new, authentic, Christ-inspired seership exemplified by the figure of Theodora in Rudolf Steiner's first mystery play (see the words of Theodora on pages 102–103). The visions of Estelle Isaacson presented in

---

72 The similarity between the stages of the trials during the 3½ years of the Antichrist and the three days of Mary Magdalene's initiation, as described by Estelle Isaacson in *Through the Eyes of Mary Magdalene*, vol. 2, pp. 20–37, would seem to indicate that there is evidently a parallel between the two initiation processes.

73 Isaacson, *Through the Eyes of Mary Magdalene*.

74 Ibid., vol. 2, pp. 233–236, 242–254. Isaacson's description of the Resurrection is one of the deepest and most profound achievements in the entire history of spiritual literature.

the following chapters, as they are inspirational, can be read many times. They have the capacity to invoke the presence of Kalki–Maitreya, the annihilator of ignorance/bearer of the Good.[75]

---

75 Note concerning chapter 1 of this book: it is a considerably expanded version of Robert Powell's article "2014 and the Coming of the Kalki Avatar," *Journal for Star Wisdom 2014.*

2

THE BODHISATTVA WHO WILL BECOME THE MAITREYA BUDDHA

I saw the bodhisattva appear, radiantly sitting in a gesture of peaceful compassion. His robes were emanating pure white light and his head was golden—as if made of gold. He drew very near and then gave the following message: Wisdom has brought you here today[1] to receive a message.

There is now present one of the twelve bodhisattvas, one who is drawing near at this moment. This bodhisattva is inhabiting—overlighting—the community of which you are a part.

You shall not be without divine guidance or protection; for the angels who serve the most holy ones are gathering around. They already know their work and have already been called. The bodhisattvas are preparing for what is coming and the angels that serve them are gathering for their work.

Your thoughts and meditations on the life of this bodhisattva bring him ever closer to you. He is the one who shall appear as the Maitreya Buddha. He can already appear in his form as the Maitreya—the Bringer of the Good—to those who are prepared to receive him now.

There are forerunners who are called to work with him now—to prepare the way for him to manifest as the Maitreya Buddha in the future. For this great one to manifest himself as the "Bringer of the Good" requires the preparation of many souls. Just as a

---

1   February 12, 2013.

great cathedral requires even the simplest stone worker—the one who knows where to find the stone and is able to bring it out of the mountain so that a great cathedral can be erected according to the vision of the one who directs its creation—so also do those great souls (even Jesus Christ and the Buddha and others) need the preparation of many souls to help bring about the manifestation of their incarnation. Likewise it is so, even with one who is great and powerful like the Maitreya Buddha. Thus he who shall be the Maitreya Buddha calls his servants and helpers; for them the Maitreya is already beginning to come now into being, so that they can have a direct experience with him before he appears in his future incarnation on the Earth as the Maitreya Buddha.

This Being was indeed Father Abraham, and out of that incarnation as Abraham some three thousand years ago came the world's great religions that are now in conflict. A great war is coming out of the seed of Abraham. This can be seen as one religion fighting against another. The children of Israel shall rage against the children of Ishmael. And included in the house of Israel there is the religion of the Jews and the Christian religion.

Even the Antichrist himself, in part, is of the line of Abraham—but only in part, for there is an element that does not come through Abraham.

Woe unto the children of Abraham.

The Maitreya shall work upon the Abrahamic stream.

It is possible through working directly with this being to bring about much good—to bring light to the conflict. In order for the Maitreya to manifest in the future, there must be resolution between these streams: Israel and Ishmael.

What is happening now in the world, and what is coming this year, is very important for the mission of the Maitreya Buddha. Those who succumb to fear are not able to work with the Maitreya. He is the bringer of the Good. He shall bring forth the Good through the raw materials available to him. He cannot take fears and weave them into paradise; he does not take violence and weave it into peace. He takes works of faith and weaves the greater good. He weaves in spiritual community that is gathered together out of love. He is not present in fear-based community. He *is* the Good. He brings the Good. He accepts the smallest offerings and through these manifests the greater Good.

Some individuals have been chosen to receive these things now; they are some of the few who have created space in their hearts for the Maitreya. Whereas Abraham's seed was great, the Maitreya's seed is young and his numbers are few. He looks the world over and finds only a very small number of souls whom he can now call to his work.

If you think of him, you are called. If you love him, you are called. The words he has spoken in the past, in other lifetimes, are words of wisdom that you are able to make your own.

Again, you must understand that the manifestation of a Great One requires much preparatory work to be done, by many souls. Those who are called are also the bringers of the Good, for they shall help to bring the Maitreya; and it is during the current world conflict that they are now able to hold to the Good and work in prayer and meditation with the Maitreya.

Meditate upon the Platonic virtues: wisdom, temperance, and courage, which together bring about righteousness. As you develop these three virtues in a greater way you will aid the work of the Maitreya, just like the stoneworker who stone-by-stone was able to assist in building the great cathedral.

The Maitreya shall appear as a being formed out of wisdom-filled Cosmic Thoughts that have been born from human souls. He will receive his form as if woven out of the Cosmic Ether of the most righteous and benevolent human thoughts. He will have the power of the greatest and most righteous human thoughts. This is why when you strive to lift your thoughts to a higher plane, ennobling them, you are helping to build up the body of the Maitreya—and he begins to manifest when enough human thoughts have become ennobled by the power of the Nine Beatitudes spoken by Christ at the Sermon on the Mount. Then shall the Maitreya appear in his full form and he shall utter the Word born out of the Cosmic Thoughts, and the Good shall instantly manifest.

He shall manifest the power of human thought. He will embody righteousness—it will become his form. He can manifest the Good in any situation, even now, if there is just one person who can think the thoughts of Goodness. You have opportunities now to put this into practice—to think the good thoughts even when you are tempted to do otherwise. You have the power to bring love to any situation, or to people who do not seem to merit it. See the challenges before you as opportunities and tests to practice bringing love, through bringing the Good. You will be inspired and you will be guided as long as you do not give in to fear. This is only a moment in eternity. This moment will be over soon. Your suffering will be the suffering of one who loves—not the suffering of one who has been overtaken by dark powers. You love, and this love will become a source of suffering. No matter what comes, continue to love!

It would be strengthening and wonderful to bring the Maitreya more fully into your community by holding times for prayers and meditations, studying his words—and in any other ways to which you are guided.

3

THE POWER OF HUMAN GOODNESS

The one who is to be the Maitreya drew near to me. A deep sense of peace came over me as I received the following message regarding his work:

THE SHADOW SIDE OF UNIFICATION

Within the field of this bodhisattva's influence lie answers and solutions to today's problems. This bodhisattva carries within him the promise of the resurrection of creation. One can endeavor to reside within this individuality's field of influence and to forge a strong connection with him. One can be within the field of his influence, and thereby one is able to receive from him guidance and inspiration.

His people are hidden, quiet, and humble. They are not known in the world, even as the individuality who shall become the Maitreya is not known in the world. As the Maitreya, he shall bring together the goodness out of the nations, out of the religions; he shall bring this together, unified in one great whole. The world, however, is not yet ready for this kind of unification.

At this time, the shadow side of the ideal of unification is manifesting. This can be seen in the many programs that attempt to make everything uniform, such as educational programs. And the world will need to go through a period of this shadow unification before finally accepting what the Maitreya is bringing. He is bringing true peace and harmony through embracing diversity and the inherent goodness that is everywhere in all peoples.

The Maitreya is the Bringer of the Good. He is taking form, emerging out of human righteousness and benevolent thoughts. Now is the time to choose the thoughts that will serve the future of the world and humanity, and to practice those thoughts.

For evil to accomplish its goals, it needs two things. It needs a victim and it needs an observer, someone who can observe and judge the deed to be evil. Evil gains its power through the victimization *and* through the observation. To reduce the effects or the power that dark forces can have over you, you must refuse to be a victim and refuse to observe evil victimizing you. The evil one can gain no power in your life if you refuse to play the role of victim. The one who brings evil does not want the Bringer of the Good to come.

Just as the Maitreya's form will emerge out of human righteousness—benevolent thoughts—so can the evil one also gain form out of the fears and hate of human beings. This is his source of power.

THE WORK OF PEACE: THE WORK OF TRANSFORMING EVIL

There will be some called to dwell in a state of goodness and peace, to hold to the ideals of peace and love in a profound way. They will live in this condition, even while the evil one reigns on the Earth. These are they who are called to live in peace so that the consciousness of peace and love is never lost from the Earth. This will be their work. They will work with the one who shall be the Maitreya.

Then there are those who are called to the work of transforming evil. They are the ones who will witness and come to an understanding of evil. Only then will they be able to transform it.

Sustaining both of these groups are many angels who will strengthen, support, and inspire. To work in these two groups requires special initiations. To remain in a state of peace while the world is in turmoil requires certain initiations. And truly, in order to transform evil, one must be initiated and called.

The peaceful way will always be present in some form on the Earth. There is always a possibility of peace. And there is always a potential for peaceful communities to exist on the Earth. One will find oneself in the community that one is called to be in, with which one resonates and can truly serve. It may not be a physical community. Its members may be spread out across the world to serve a higher purpose. In what way, in one's heart of hearts, would one most want to serve? Is it perhaps to assist in holding peace during this time of transition? If this is one's heart's wish and one feels this as a calling, one can open oneself to learning the way of peace.

One can also endeavor to understand the value of peace. On a deeper level this is to know Gautama Buddha. And perhaps it is part of one's work to build a bridge between the ancient Buddha and the future Buddha, in terms of human evolution, so that many can be prepared for the new consciousness that the coming Buddha shall bring.

THE SECOND COMING OF CHRIST: PREPARATION FOR THE MAITREYA

The One being who stands at the turning point, between the two, is Christ in his Second Coming. Those who can learn and follow the great teachings of the Buddha and accept the teachings of Christ—who appears now in the realm of the Earth's etheric-formative forces—will be prepared for the Maitreya. The Second Coming of Christ heralds in a special way the coming of the Maitreya Buddha. This is why these times (the current time-frame and what is coming in the near future) are all-important for the Christ, who is now present in the etheric realm and is able to bring about great transformation in souls. It is a transformation that prepares human beings for the work of the Maitreya. Thus, in our time, the work with the Etheric Christ relates directly to the future activity of the Maitreya Buddha.

When the Maitreya comes, he will bring about a restoration of the Eternal Good, which belongs to the body of the Earth. All of the goodness that was taken in by Christ is dwelling now in the etheric body of the Earth. Not only did he take upon himself sin and suffering, he also bore our goodness. That goodness can be accessed at any time by human beings who, out of purity of heart, can hold to and retain their faith in humanity's goodness. The Maitreya will bring this human goodness to light and manifest it in physical reality.

Who does not believe in human goodness? Who has no faith in human beings? This is the Antichrist. The Antichrist can never have power over human beings who can see and love the goodness in the other. The Maitreya will be a blessing to the Earth, for he will restore to human beings the powers of seeing and knowing the goodness. Human beings by this time will have gone through the great trial that is the temptation to lose faith in others, and even to lose faith in the goodness of one's own self. One strengthens the forces of goodness in the Earth by holding always to noble thoughts of others and seeing the good in everything that happens. Any detrimental or destructive force can be transformed into a beneficial, life-supporting force through love. Working with the Christ means aligning with the power of the good. Thereby strength is attained, through which—if one is called to such a work—the power of goodness may be brought to bear upon evil and eventually may even transform evil, so that it returns to alignment with goodness. The key point here is that the alignment with Christ has to be strong enough; then the force of goodness can radiate into evil so powerfully that the latter yields and becomes subordinate to the strength of goodness. It should be noted, however, that the transformation of evil into good is a specialized calling, which can only be undertaken safely when the individual is truly called to take up such a work on a spiritual basis.

It is important to study the words of the Maitreya. And one can think of oneself as a part of him, as a microcosm—or even as an early embryo—of his being. By aligning oneself with him now, one is contributing to the work of bringing forth the good that is already present and making it known to others. Wherever one sees what is uplifting, righteous and good, this is the impulse of the Maitreya already at work. For example, there are those journalists who decide to stop reporting the heinous, ugly things and instead report the *good* news; they are working under the inspiration of the Maitreya. They are generating more of the good. No effort is too small in this regard. One's efforts in this respect have tremendous power. Peace shines through the good.

Another wonderful example of a servant, a forerunner for the Maitreya, is Mother Theresa, who could see the beautiful being dwelling under the chaos of leprosy. In that kind of beholding, true healing and transformation can happen.

There is so much goodness in the hearts of people. Yes, we must give a glance and acknowledge what the dark side is doing; but more significantly, we must not give up faith in humanity. There is always a higher perspective that goes beyond the illusions of this world. This life is short and eternity looms ahead. Some things that now seem so important will lose their importance in the light of eternity. One can endeavor to bring one's focus to the present time, where there is enough goodness to bring about great joy today, right here and now.[1]

---

1   This vision was given on February 28, 2013.

4

ALIGN WITH ME
AND THINK THE GOOD THOUGHTS

There are some who are called to the work of *Peace*, to maintain inner peace through whatever comes. Everyone, potentially, has the power to restore inner peace. Elevating one's thoughts above the finite plane of this singular earthly existence leads to the perspective that this life is only a day in eternity. There is tomorrow, and there are many tomorrows. If one brings oneself back to one's center and refocuses on the blessed task at hand, this life—this day in eternity—opens up. Let one's heart travel by love. If one wants to move into a different life situation, and the objective and the planning are a source of love, then the way will be opened. If there is an impulse of love and a calling in the heart, then one will be able to accomplish this calling.

The one who will become the Maitreya Buddha knows his small group of disciples and he is *known* by them. He is watching over the ones who know him, for he is preparing *through* them—through their hearts—for his life when he shall appear as the Maitreya. His disciples are doing the work to prepare for him.

He appears to inner vision as a sitting Buddha, radiantly white, his head golden, filled with thoughts of the Good—all the Good thoughts of human beings and angels. He holds for his disciples, and for all others, the ideals of the Good, the True, and the Beautiful, even while here on the Earth there is the rumbling of degenerated thoughts and evil feelings plaguing the human condition.

Human beings are now being told *what* to think in order to generate the most fear. Programs of anxiety are being sent around the globe. It is not a matter merely of general anxiety, for these programs have the ability, once settling into the human field, to become personal to each individual. Thus it is that people everywhere may begin to feel anxiety and may become trapped in their feelings. The Maitreya, however, offers a remedy.

He says to all: Align with me. Think Good thoughts, feel Good feelings, and let Good will prevail.

Through him—as he is aligned with Christ in the Etheric—True and Good thoughts and Beautiful feelings are available as a remedy to those destructive programs being generated by the evil one. The evil one gains his power through fear and negative thinking and the ensuing forgetting of Love on the part of human beings. *This is a process that contributes to the development of his body.*

Likewise, the Maitreya receives his body from the benevolent thoughts of those human beings who are able to awaken and say, "I will not think these thoughts; I will think the thoughts of the Good."

Some are called to see and behold what is truly happening in the world. These individuals must learn to think the Good thoughts even while beholding evil deeds.

The body of the Maitreya is being formed NOW, and this will continue over the course of many generations, even as the children of Israel were required to live the Law of Moses in order to bring about the ideal body for Christ to indwell. It was Christ who directed the creation of his own body. Now the Maitreya does likewise. It is his little group of disciples that is the image of his light. For, indeed, he shall come through a lineage not of blood, but of light.

For all who are called to his work, this is a very important time. By thinking thoughts of the Good, one does the work of the

Maitreya, who will be able to take those Good thoughts and bring forth the Good on Earth. He will bring to pass the physical manifestation of the spiritual creations now underway by those beings who are thinking Good thoughts.

Blessed are those who can think the thoughts of the angelic realm.

Blessed are those who are invited to work with the Maitreya.

One's own personal life questions are the perfect ground for one to take up the work of the Maitreya. Just as the evil one desires to take over individual souls to sow seeds of doubt, despair, and anxiety, so that he can build up a more powerful body for himself—know also that the Maitreya, even though he will not become the Maitreya Buddha in physical incarnation for many generations, can work with one on a personal level.

Those individuals who become truly free, masters of their own souls, have the power to change the world. One's own life is indeed important. The task that one feels called to do in the world *is* important. One can offer one's life in service to the Maitreya's work, and *ask* him for the strength to think the thoughts of the Good.

And he shall be with you.[1]

---

1   This vision was given on March 2, 2013.

5

THE MAITREYA: TRAVERSING THE ABYSS

The following is a message from the one who shall become the Maitreya Buddha.[1]

Thus he spoke:

It has been my task and my joy to usher the souls of humanity into their awakening. I have stood in those places, in those points of time, wherein it was needful that one could help to carry souls across the Great Abyss. I have stood at the edge of the abyss. I am one who knows the abyss. I know what lies on the other side. And I know the way by which the abyss may be traversed. I have been present during many crucial times in the history of the world and have held up a beacon of light to show the way, to reveal the path to the Christ.

Throughout all of my incarnations I have been preparing for the time when I shall come as the Maitreya Buddha.

I have been able to understand the Great Abyss from many different perspectives, and have discovered that it is possible to triumph over evil—which every human being has the power within to overcome—and that it is also possible to *transform* evil. This is done through the power of love. This is the wisdom that flows in my being, wisdom which may be given to those who truly seek to take up this task. Together with the Christ Being this work may be first accomplished in individual souls. And then these souls may work to accomplish this on the Earth.

---

1   Given on May 21, 2013.

To become an agent of transformation, one must find the peace that surpasses all understanding. And to make order out of chaos, one must strive for inner order. This state of inner order is achieved through right meditation, right thinking, right speaking, and right walking.

Through communion with Christ, as you take in his sacred substance, your being will become ever more ordered.

There is much distraction in this world. The distractions will only increase. Yes, there are good diversions—so-called positive things—which distract. Keep your focus on where it is you know you are to go, and reduce the distractions. Let go of the inessential.

And when you meet a trial, you must ask questions. The trial brings up pain. The pain is the door. Numbing the pain closes the door. And the key to the door, the door of Eternal Life, lies within you. You must ask the proper questions when facing a trial. You will know when you have found the right question, for it shall resound within your being. And then you will be able to place this question on the altar. This is a practice which my disciples shall take up, facing a trial as an *opportunity*. If you allow yourself to succumb to complaining, resistance, and anger, then you will miss an opening; for the trial is an opening to a higher level. Not all can be revealed regarding this; but for those who desire to be my disciples, I ask you to bring your full presence to that door—the door that *is* the trial. And I invite you to ask the right question. Teach this principle to any who are going through a trial. The one who passes the test is the one who is humble, empty, trusting. And when this door is opened you shall receive a gift.

This will be a training, one by which you can learn to think true thoughts, good thoughts, even while going through a trial. There is tremendous power in this. This is the sharpening of the sword. The sword can only be sharpened through the power of the true Word. And one must find the true Word if one's own sword is to be sharpened. And the true Word arises out of the question that is borne from your spirit. Then you shall have the power to cast out the evil or transform the evil, if it chooses to be transformed.

Blessings to you all. Go forth in faith and peace, and never doubt.

6

When the Maitreya Buddha Comes

The Future World of the Maitreya

As the vision began, I soon found myself hovering above the Earth in a future time. I descended very slowly toward the Earth. Conditions had changed so much that I felt cautious in my approach. The Earth appeared dull, lacking the vibrancy that I have seen in the past when gazing down from a distance. Thick clouds filled the atmosphere, covering the Earth.

As I came to rest on the Earth, I beheld a woman whose face was strong and robust with kind, compassionate eyes. Her lips were full and her skin was a medium shade of brown. She wore a light grey hooded tunic. The long-sleeved garment was simple in construction and fell to the knees. On her feet were curious boots in a light grey color.

In her society she was called the Speaker. She was the one who watched the heavens and received messages for the community. This community of good people had separated from the larger society and was living a nomadic life in the mountains. They worked together to hear and receive the word of God and to carry this word in their hearts during the dark times.

This woman was able to find a place in the mountains where the oppressive atmosphere had some breaks in it, where sometimes the stars could be seen. And it was there that she found she could receive angelic communications. It was there that she received, on the mountaintop, the vision of the Prince of the Highest Good.

She was gazing into the sky. The clouds were impenetrable and ominous. She waited. The clouds stirred and gathered and the vision began. She saw a huge hand descend out of the clouds. In the palm of the hand was a babe. He appeared as if formed from the clouds, yet he was luminous. He was dressed in a most curious garb: a pleated kilt-like skirt with a jeweled band at the waist, and a strap leading diagonally from the waist across his chest, also jeweled. His hair was dark and curly and he had large, loving eyes. A voice proclaimed, "Behold the babe! See what he does for humankind!" The woman was told that she was to observe all that this child did, throughout his life, and to be a witness for him. She was to care for him, but she understood that God was to be his "true" parent.

❀

After seeing this woman's vision, I was told that this babe was the Kalki Avatar, also known as the Maitreya Buddha, and that he shall be born in the far distant future into a royal line, into a world wallowing in darkness. At that time, the Christ will have been forgotten in most minds. Only a few groups of human beings will have been able to remember and know the Christ.

There will be cities that will have become completely mechanized, engendering a "machine" existence in which nothing spiritual thrives and there are no longer feelings of true joy or happiness. Human beings living in these cities will have become part of this existence. Their "I" will be so far removed that they will have become mostly astral in nature, having degenerated to the level of the animal kingdom where astral urges and desires are acted out without any conscience. Sub-earthly forces will have taken them over, so that what was once a mystery—the unknowable depths of the sub-terrestrial levels—will have become reality in certain places on the surface of the Earth.

Murder will be acceptable there. Not a single commandment will be upheld. Chaos and disorder will reign and the people will have become ugly. Yet, a power will exist in them that is not now known in our world. It is a secret power, which will become prevalent in that future time. It is a power that artificially sustains life and gives great physical power as well as a keen cleverness—not true enlightened thinking as intellect, but a debased cleverness, like unto the cleverness of some animals. In that future time this will have become a power that takes over the mind and lends a super-human quality that all people want, and everything will be done to cultivate this power. All will live in fear because of this power. This will be the worst of the worst, for there will be no beauty to be seen. The Earth in those areas will be raped for Her minerals, which will be given to the machine; and the process by which these minerals are leached out of the Earth will be damning to Nature. The Breath of Life will not be found there, and the only plant life to be found will be what has been taken over by the evil one to serve its goal. The plant life there will be harsh, bitter, and dense in its structure. It will produce drugs. These plants will be grown in laboratory-like facilities under lock and key, so to speak. They will be used to feed the animal-humans, whereby their lowly astral urges will be strengthened. Through these plants the dark forces will control the masses over whom they wield their power.

There will be other societies, which will not be quite so degenerate. These will be the ones oppressed by the power of the aforementioned cities. They too will have lost their connection to Spirit, but will not have given themselves over to the utterly decadent way of being, and will not be directly part of the machine of the evil one. They will live in unconsciousness and all of their life energy will be focused upon survival.

There will also be the societies of the Good. Their numbers will be relatively small. They will be hidden throughout the world in centers of light. They will know that one is coming who will bring about great change for the Earth and humanity. They will await his coming.

THE GREAT AWAKENING

I then saw the Maitreya. He is of the most pure, golden light, emanating profound peace. He imbued me with his light.

This woman of the future, whom I mentioned before, will have the ability to connect Heaven and Earth, to be a channel between the two during the time leading up to the incarnation of the Maitreya, when Heaven and Earth will have become so separated from most human beings. What she receives from the Earth and from Heaven will be united in her heart. Her task will be to bear the human predicament to the Hierarchies through the Archangel with whom she works. She will be a human channel for the plan of the Hierarchies to be fulfilled on Earth; for, through her, the antidote for the human predicament may be received and may unfold as consciousness on the earthly plane. This is how the Maitreya will be able to come, descending at the right time and in the right place. He will know that it is time to come when the Hierarchies have received the human predicament into their own beings. This will happen through the aid of this woman who is able to communicate with Heaven. Through the Archangel, she is able to communicate with the Elohim. Her life's task is to be an observer on behalf of Heaven—to observe Earthly evolution through her human perspective and offer this beholding to the Hierarchies.

The being of the Maitreya spoke:

"The Good shall dwell in you through all things that will come. You will never lose the Good. You will know the Good henceforth. And the Good shall be your strength and your protection, and you shall be the seeker of the Good. When I come, I will awaken the Good in the sleeping souls, and you may assist me in this work. And the Good shall be remembered in them.

"The woman who is to be my mother shall call me into existence when the time is right. She shall bring me forth by the power of the Word. It will be a Word that has never yet been spoken, a Word that shall be spoken between Heaven and Earth. And the Word shall bring me forth and I will be born to the woman who shall observe all that I do. And by the power of her observation, the Hierarchies shall work in me.

"And out of the Good, I will call my disciples from the righteous; and I will have many, many disciples. They will have the power of the Good. A great awakening shall happen in the righteous societies.

"Before my coming, the societies of the Good will have become completely removed from the degenerate societies. For many generations they will have lived separately. They will have lived in peace and beauty. Their elders shall speak of legends: tales of the evil that once existed on the Earth. Legends of the evil will abound in the societies of the Good. The peaceful people will believe that the time of evil was something of the deep past. These societies will be located in hidden places on the Earth.

"But when the time is right for the Great Awakening, there shall be some youth who hear the legends and believe that the evil communities do indeed exist somewhere. They will decide to go and search. They will feel in their hearts that it is not right that there should be human beings living in utter darkness while they themselves live in the light. They will want to become saviors for the dark ones. The elders will tell them not to go, that these are just legends—that it is not necessary to go and search. But the youth will have the strongest urge to go out, and so they will leave. After many fruitless journeys, they will eventually find these societies that have so degenerated. And they will go through many trials, many spiritual trials, when the discovery is made. For everything that they knew will now be thrown into upheaval. They will be initiated into the knowledge of evil, observing evil in its many forms; and they will have to battle for their own souls, so that they do not succumb and become lost. After many trials they will return to the people of the light and report to them. And then all hearts will be overcome by a great grieving. All hearts of the peaceful ones will be broken by this knowledge; no longer will these people be able to dwell in blissful ignorance. They will then have to work for the redemption of the degenerate Earth and humanity. The ancient legends of the Second Coming of the Christ will be restored and revisited. And the very ancient legend of Christ's sacrifice on Golgotha will be restored and returned to full consciousness. These most crucial times in Earth history will be revisited and the question will then arise, 'We have now awakened to the unredeemed. What now must we do to bring truth and beauty and goodness into these dark places on the Earth?'

"And this awakening, then, will be the fertile ground that is prepared before my coming. The people of the light will be made ready to receive me. And then my work of bringing the Good to the whole Earth shall commence. And I shall come by the power of the Word, the Word that is sacred magic, spoken at the right time by one who is the speaker of the Good."

❧

And this woman who was called the Speaker—she is one who will hear the reports of the youth. It will awaken in her that she should take a band of people and go into the mountains to find out what must be done. It is then that she will be given the vision of the Maitreya's coming. And there is much to say about the things she and this band of people will experience. But these stories are for another time.

The power of the Good is ever present and dwells in human hearts. Let the power of the Good be your guide, that you may be filled with the grace and love of God, and that you may be protected in all that you do.

The Maitreya speaks, "I am the Manifestor of the Good. I shall manifest the Good through you and the Good will prevail on Earth. All virtues stream forth from the heart that is filled with goodness. Each of the virtues is a sacred power. And these powers are for the transformation of the Earth. These are the virtues inherent in the nine Beatitudes spoken by Christ. Hold to these powers and keep them sacred, and you shall be blessed. Amen."[1]

---

1   This vision was given on August 30, 2013.

7

THE ETERNAL SMILE

THE FUTURE WORLD OF THE MAITREYA

I saw the one who will be the Maitreya. When the Maitreya comes he will have the power to embody his disciples; and when he appears now, in his current form, he may do this to a certain extent. For those who seek in righteousness to know him, he can dwell within their heart.

The Maitreya showed me a vision,[1] saying:

"If we are to arrive somewhere, we must be able to envision where we are going. If you plan a trip to Paris, for instance, it is best to learn everything you can about Paris and its people and culture so that you are prepared when you arrive." I was then given a vision of the future when the Maitreya Buddha will be present in body on the Earth.

First I shall describe the Maitreya. I am certain that this being is of a feminine quality when manifested—however he is perfectly balanced in the male/female energy. The beauty of the Maitreya Buddha is so unfathomable! He is like unto a community of great beings in and of himself. A train of glory leads out from him, of all the great souls who prepared the way for him to manifest. This is his train of glory, these great souls who will dwell within the Maitreya's spiritual bodies. They will assist in the Maitreya's great work. They are the ones who have been called *bodhisattvas*, and each brings a gift to the Maitreya Buddha's incarnation. A

---

1   Given on April 5, 2013.

multifaceted being, the Maitreya is very highly evolved. I lack the words to describe his spiritual form, for I have not yet seen such a highly evolved *human* being.

The Maitreya Buddha will have the ability to call upon the powers of the elements, elemental powers. But because of great purity and wisdom he will use those powers only in the most noble and benevolent ways. The individuality of the Maitreya will have had access to those powers in prior lifetimes and will have learned the true way—the noble and moral way of working with the elements. He will lift the elements to a higher level through his work.

The Maitreya will be able to create through the power of the Word. He will speak into existence higher creation. In this way, Nature will be able to claim its redemption. His disciples shall perform this work also—the work of redeeming Nature. He will re-establish the connection between Heaven and Earth. Nature will be lifted into a higher spiritual existence. The angelic realm will be able to work more closely with Nature, much more so than it does now.

And the human beings who know the Maitreya, and who join themselves in his impulse, will eventually transform—becoming more like human angels. He will have his dominion and his dominion is now being prepared. The dominion of the Maitreya includes all beings who know him and want to join in his work.

This message and vision is coming for all and for those who have specific tasks with the Maitreya. You have been called. The Maitreya shall touch your hearts and awaken gifts in you. And there are others who belong to his community. His community is already present in the etheric realm in which your hearts are connected. You are preparers of the way.

Look at what a benevolent thought can do! Look at what can be created by the power of your thoughts. When you align your thoughts with the being of the Maitreya, look at what your thoughts can create! See the great City that is coming to the Earth, the City that is coming.[2] Think the thoughts of this City. Think the Maitreya's thoughts, his thoughts of peace; think the thoughts of the peaceful heart. The great heart of peaceful humanity *will* prevail on Earth. The Maitreya will give to you the peaceful heart so that you may think the good thoughts, the thoughts that will bring him into incarnation. He is born through the good thoughts of the peaceful hearts. Receive the Maitreya's heart. Bear his heart in you.

So unspeakable are the goodness and the beauty of this great Being! He is coming from the golden realm of Shambhala. He works from there even now upon the sub-earthly layers, performing the work of transformation. And he will call to his disciples to aid in the work of transformation, to hold in their hearts his heart of peace, and to bring that peace into the darkest places so that the darkness may be transformed. Darkness may be illuminated and transformed by the light of heavenly peace. And this is the Maitreya's work.

His people shall live and move and think and create by the power of goodness and love. They will be able to transport themselves by the wings of the love that they will come to know through their communion with the Maitreya. They will not be so limited by time or space. His community will be a community of freedom, such as has never been known on this Earth. Those belonging to his community will be free to move, to act, between Heaven and Earth. They will have the power of the Word, that by their word there shall be creation.

In joining his etheric community, your word becomes imbued with power, and perhaps already has power. Place your word and the power therein on the altar to be used by the Maitreya and his spiritual community to bring about creation. Think in concert with his community now. It is by your righteous thoughts that

2   This City, known as the Heavenly Jerusalem, comprises the New Earth, the Earth spiritualized through Christ's sacrifice, and the New Heaven borne down from celestial heights by the Bride of the Lamb, Sophia.

you travel and shall then find yourself in his community. It is not by physical vehicle that you shall arrive. You shall arrive there by thought—pure, benevolent, spirit-filled thought. You have the power to travel in this manner. This is the secret of his gathering. This gathering is by love, in love. The peaceful hearts shall transform the Earth. Think with the Maitreya and dwell in his goodness and he will be able to indwell your heart until that time when his one body, the true body of his incarnation shall manifest. Until then his disciples will embody aspects of his being.

THE ETERNAL SMILE

You are the wombs that will carry the Maitreya into existence. Your bodies, your spiritual bodies, are the pillars of the great temple. And the temple is not empty, but is filled with his light and becomes the beacon of light, the temple of light in the City on the hill, which beckons to all:

Come unto me, O precious Sons and Daughters of Light!
Bring your light to my temple and let it shine for all to see.
I claim you as my disciples in the secret places of your heart.
I will enlighten your heart and transform it that it becomes
    a temple of peace.

I am the Eternal Smile of Shambhala.
I am the golden warmth at the heart of the Earth.
I am the healing elixir for souls.
I am the heart of ineffable peace.
I am the Good Thought and the bringer of all righteousness.
I am the jewel at the heart of the lotus.
Peace. Peace. Peace.

I am smiling through your entire soul.
Give my smile to others.
Greet every being with my smile.
Let my smile heal all.
You are the bearers of my Eternal Smile.

And this is my work, to bring smiles to the faces of all
    children.
Join with me in my work of spreading the Eternal Smile
    throughout the world.

Go in peace, smiling disciples.

I will be with you. I will be in you.

Namasté.

RUDOLF STEINER ON
THE MAITREYA BUDDHA AND THE KALKI AVATAR

In light of Rudolf Steiner's remarks, the year 2014 is indicated to be a very significant point of transition in the unfolding of spiritual evolution. This is discussed in detail in my article "2014 and the Coming of the Kalki Avatar,"[1] the first chapter in this book, as it provides important material for understanding the significance of the year 2014 in humanity's spiritual history. Also in this book is an article by Estelle Isaacson titled "The Bodhisattva Who Will Become the Maitreya Buddha."[2] This article derives from a profound vision that Estelle Isaacson had on February 12, 2013, concerning this bodhisattva, whose name (Maitreya) means "bearer of the Good." This bodhisattva, the successor to Gautama Buddha, is spoken of in numerous lectures by Rudolf Steiner as a great spiritual teacher and leader of humankind, as discussed later in this appendix. At this juncture, as presented in the foreword and in chapter one of this book, it is helpful to consider that the Maitreya Buddha who is awaited as the next Buddha in Buddhism is one and the same as the Kalki Avatar, the next avatar awaited in Hinduism.

Interestingly, Steiner spoke of the Kalki Avatar only once—in his first esoteric lesson, held in Berlin in the summer of 1903

---

1   Powell, "2014 and the Coming of the Kalki Avatar," *Journal for Star Wisdom 2014*, pp. 22–35.

2   Isaacson, "The Bodhisattva who will become the Maitreya Buddha," *Journal for Star Wisdom 2014*, pp. 36–37; see chapter 2 of this book.

(precise date unknown). In order to provide the reader with some background concerning Kalki, I have translated the following passages from this first esoteric lesson, which bears the title: "The Solar Logos and the Ten Avatars."[3]

The holy books of the Vedas and the Rosicrucian Chronicle[4] speak of ten such avatars or metamorphoses of our present Solar Logos.... The Solar Logos incarnates as archetype and leader at [each] new phase of evolution.... Christ was for the Rosicrucians this *coming one*. [In this esoteric lesson Rudolf Steiner describes the first six avatars of Hinduism and then comes to the seventh avatar, Rama, quoting from the Rosicrucian Chronicle]: "The compelling nature of the spirit being was profundity and severity. Then, from itself, it gave birth to mildness. The severe commandment of the law dissolved into love." Then came Krishna, the eighth avatar [quoting from the Rosicrucian Chronicle]: "And the seed of love blossomed and bore the fruit of love called blessedness. And the human being was blessedness." Then the ninth avatar, Buddha, appeared as both guide and archetype [quoting from the Rosicrucian Chronicle]: "And blessedness sent her son to the Earth, the one who is known as 'incarnated wisdom.' And she dwelt in the dying body of the son of the king"—Buddha. The tenth avatar is the *coming one*: Kalki, according to the Indian [sources]. The Rosicrucian Chronicle states: "However, when the times are fulfilled, the eye opens, and human destiny is illumined inwardly. Choose the radiant figure as leader: then destiny itself will be for you law and loving will. For the one whose eye opens will see living roses growing from the cross."

Given the significance of Kalki, and considering the identity of this avatar with the Maitreya, much can be learned about this

---

3   Steiner, *Über die astrale Welt und das Devachan* (On the Astral World and Devachan, CW 88), pp. 149–154; notes in brackets [ ] inserted by R.P.

4   This is the only occasion on which Steiner uses the expression "Rosicrucian Chronicle," which from the context clearly refers to a kind of "Rosicrucian Akashic Chronicle," which Steiner was able to read.

great spiritual leader—in addition to the above communication—
by contemplating Rudolf Steiner's indications concerning the bodhisattva who will become the Maitreya Buddha. One can read the
full context of these indications in his lecture cycles on the Gospel
of St. Luke and the Gospel of St. Matthew.

❁

Before coming to the relevant quotes from these lecture cycles it
is, however, important to consider some guidelines—four basic
points: (a), (b), (c), (d), followed by a fifth point (e)—intended as an
aid to steer through the wealth of communications given by Steiner.

(a) A bodhisattva is a human being—one of a group of twelve—
who is of such a high level of spiritual development that he or
she is capable of being the bearer of an Archangel—noting that
Archangels are the guardian spirits guiding groups and peoples,
just as Angels serve as the guardian spirits of individuals in the
unfolding of their destiny. Since an Archangel is the guardian
spirit of an entire group or people, a bodhisattva can potentially
inspire a whole community of people. A classic historical example
of a bodhisattva is Moses, who, as indicated implicitly by Steiner
in section [3] a bit further along in this text, was one of the twelve
bodhisattvas, as also were Abraham and Elijah. As Steiner indicates, the Archangel Michael was the Folk Spirit (Archangel) of
the people of Ancient Israel. "The Folk Spirit which united with
Moses at his initiation and then dwelt in him was Michael....
Moses was united with Michael at his initiation. He now became
the group soul of his people."[5] Against this background we can
understand the overriding significance of Moses for the people
of Israel, in that—as a bodhisattva—he was the bearer of the
Archangel Michael, who was the Folk Spirit of that people. It is of
interest, as indicated in chapter one, that also Rudolf Steiner was
a bodhisattva.

---

5   Steiner, *"Freemasonry" and Ritual Work*, pp. 443–444.

(b) The focus of attention in this book is on the bodhisattva who was the successor of Gautama Buddha. *Successor*—this means to say, the bodhisattva who will be the next Buddha, known as the Maitreya Buddha. As Steiner points out, this bodhisattva has incarnated again and again in the course of the centuries, and was also incarnated in the twentieth century.[6] As referred to in section [4], this bodhisattva's final incarnation will be the one in which he ascends to become the Maitreya Buddha; moreover, the Maitreya will become a Buddha exactly five thousand years after Gautama Buddha's enlightenment under the Bodhi tree. As indicated in chapter one, the Maitreya Buddha incarnation will be around the year 4443, as discussed also in my book *Hermetic Astrology,* volume 1.[7] Whereas a bodhisattva continues to incarnate upon the Earth and is capable of being the bearer of an Archangel, a Buddha no longer incarnates upon the Earth, but works from spiritual realms on the level of an Archai or Time Spirit—one rank higher than an Archangel.

It should be observed that at the time Rudolf Steiner was lecturing, he was careful to mention only one earlier incarnation of the bodhisattva who will become the Maitreya Buddha: that of Jeshu ben Pandira, the teacher of the Essenes. His teachings in that incarnation, as leader of the Essene community at Qumran by the Dead Sea, were written down on scrolls, later known as the Dead

---

6   Steiner, *From Jesus to Christ,* lecture 10, Oct. 14, 1911; in the words of
     Steiner, "Who was Jeshu ben Pandira? The successor of the bodhisattva
     who in his final earthly incarnation had risen in his twenty-ninth year
     to be Gautama Buddha was incorporated in the physical body of Jeshu
     ben Pandira.... The bodhisattva who worked at that time in preparation
     for the Christ Event was re-embodied again and again. One of his
     re-embodiments is fixed for the twentieth century."

7   Powell, *Hermetic Astrology,* vol. 1, pp. 75–84; see also p. 90, footnote
     26, for the indication concerning the birth year of Gautama as 558 BC.
     Note that there are various indications regarding the year of birth of
     Gautama, one being 558 BC, which is written in astronomical notation
     as -557. Adding five thousand years to -557, we arrive at the year 4443,
     when there will be a conjunction of Jupiter and Saturn at the end of the
     sidereal sign of Pisces.

Sea Scrolls after they were discovered in 1947 in caves close to the remains of the Essene settlement at Qumran. It would lead too far, here, to go into the background of the central teachings of Jeshu ben Pandira. One thing is clear, though: that the core essence of these teachings of Jeshu ben Pandira from the Dead Sea Scrolls—concerning the coming of a kingly messiah, a priestly messiah, and a prophet—was proclaimed by Steiner in the early twentieth century, long before the Dead Sea Scrolls were found,[8] thus showing a profound level of two bodhisattvas working together. Also, a profound level of collaboration in the twentieth century between these two individualities—Steiner and the twentieth century reincarnated Jeshu ben Pandira—is indicated by Steiner in the last part of section [2], which follows a few pages on from here.

(c) Bearing in mind the approximate date (4443) when the final incarnation of the Maitreya individuality will take place, it can be seen that for Rudolf Steiner—speaking in the years around 1910 about this coming Buddha—the event for him lay some 2,533 years in the future. In section [2] of this appendix we see that Rudolf Steiner refers to 2,500 years, which is a good approximation. In other lectures, also quoted here, he indicates that this event lies 3,000 years in the future, which is not so accurate. Perhaps 3,000 years can be thought of as a "rounding up" of 2,533 to the nearest rounded figure—i.e., 3,000.

(d) It is now important to clarify the identity of the Maitreya Buddha and the Kalki Avatar. As pointed out in chapter one, there is an absolute identity. Buddhists, talking about the future Maitreya Buddha, and Hindus discussing the future Kalki Avatar, are speaking of one and the same future historical figure—i.e., the Maitreya Buddha/Kalki Avatar in his final incarnation upon the Earth around the year 4443. It would be misleading, however,

---

8   Rau, *Die beiden Jesusknaben und die Messiaserwartung der Essener* ("The Two Jesus Children and the Essenes' Expectation of the Messiah").

to speak of the Maitreya Buddha incarnated prior to that final incarnation. In each of the incarnations (approximately one each century—see section [3]) leading up to the final incarnation, it is a matter of "the bodhisattva who will become the Maitreya Buddha." Abbreviating this, it is possible to speak of the Maitreya Bodhisattva, or simply, the Maitreya. Likewise, it would be misleading to speak of the Kalki Avatar incarnated prior to the final incarnation in approximately the year 4443. How may we designate the preceding incarnations leading up to that of the Kalki Avatar? In Hinduism there is not the concept of bodhisattva. Hence, in speaking of the "coming of the Kalki Avatar" in the year 2014, it is a matter of understanding—with the help of the Buddhist teaching concerning bodhisattvas—that in 2014 there is to be an important incarnation of the human being (the Maitreya Bodhisattva) who will become the future Maitreya Buddha/Kalki Avatar around the year 4443. The twenty-first century incarnation of this bodhisattva can be seen as part of a "wave" that keeps coming—building up from century to century—leading toward a crescendo with the incarnation of the Maitreya Buddha/Kalki Avatar around the year 4443.

(e) It can be seen that there is a vast panorama of esoteric teaching underlying the theme that is the subject matter of this book. By keeping the preceding four points in mind as a beginning, it is possible to steer one's way through the multi-layered depictions given by Rudolf Steiner in the following quotations, thereby enriching one's comprehension of this great teacher—the bodhisattva who will become the Maitreya Buddha/Kalki Avatar. There is much more that could be stated about this bodhisattva, which, however, is of such a subtle nature that it can only be properly communicated once one has truly become a disciple of this great teacher. In this respect, perhaps the most important point of all is to grasp a fundamental principle of esoteric law. Given that, as Rudolf Steiner indicated (see chapter one), the bodhisattva who will become the

Maitreya Buddha is the *actual proclaimer* of Christ in the etheric realm, it follows that *this individuality holds the key to opening the door of spiritual access to the Etheric Christ.* This is the primary and fundamental motivation for finding an inner relationship and connection with this great teacher. Ultimately, this is the reason the authors have written this book: to help readers find an inner relationship and connection with the bodhisattva who will become the Maitreya Buddha, the one who holds the key to enabling human beings to come into alignment with Christ in the etheric realm.[9]

❁

The following sections are devoted to a discussion of relevant quotes from Rudolf Steiner concerning the bodhisattva who will become the Maitreya Buddha. Translations of these indications from the German text of [1] Steiner's lecture course *The Gospel of St. Luke* are by Robert Powell, and translations of these indications from the German text of [2] Steiner's course *The Gospel of St. Matthew* are by Dorothy Osmond and Mildred Kirkcaldy (with a few minor revisions to facilitate readability):

> [1] Such beings as the bodhisattva who became Buddha, and who had the mission to incorporate into humankind the great teaching of love and compassion, stand in connection with our cosmos to which the Earth belongs. There are twelve such beings, and the bodhisattva who became Buddha five to six centuries before our era is one of these twelve. All bodhisattvas have a definite mission. Just as this one had the mission to bring the teaching of love and compassion upon the Earth, so the others have their missions, which have to be fulfilled in the various epochs of the Earth. Buddha stands particularly close to the Earth, because the development of a moral orientation is precisely the task of

---

9   Powell, *Cultivating Inner Radiance and the Body of Immortality,*
       explores this theme in detail, with practical exercises for aligning with
       the Etheric Christ.

our time—that is, from the point in time when the bodhisattva appeared five to six centuries before our era until
this bodhisattva hands over the mantle to his bodhisattva
successor, who will live upon the Earth as the Maitreya
Buddha.... We have to recognize as a lodge ruling over our
whole Earth evolution the great lodge of twelve bodhisattvas.... If you would be able to look into the great spiritual
lodge of the bodhisattvas, into the circle of the twelve bodhisattvas, you would find a thirteenth being sitting in the
midst of the twelve bodhisattvas in our world existence....
The thirteenth is the one whom the ancient Rishis named
Vishvakarma, whom Zarathustra named Ahura Mazda;
this is he whom we call Christ. And thus he stands to all
bodhisattvas; thus he is the leader and guide of the great
lodge of bodhisattvas.... In the meantime the living force
of love must stream in, so that the Maitreya Buddha finds
human beings who not only have insight into what love is,
but also have the *force* of love within them.... The successor of the Buddha, who is a bodhisattva at the present time,
is well known to those who are conversant with spiritual
science, and the time will come when these facts will be
discussed at length, whereby this bodhisattva is also to be
named—the one who will become the Maitreya Buddha....
When this bodhisattva appears on the Earth and becomes
the Maitreya Buddha, he will then find on Earth the seed
of Christ. This will be those human beings who will say:
Not only my head is filled with the wisdom of the eightfold
path [of Buddha], I have not only the teaching, the wisdom
of love, but my heart is full of the living substance of love,
which overflows and rays out into the world. With such
human beings will the Maitreya Buddha be able to continue
his mission for the further evolutionary development of the
world.[10]

[2] The two bodhisattvas—to whom reference has often been
made when we have been speaking of the evolution of humanity—of primary interest for our own times are the son of King

---

10   Steiner, *According to Luke*, lectures 7 and 9.

Suddhodana who became Buddha, and he who as Gautama Buddha's successor in the office of bodhisattva still holds this office today and—as Oriental wisdom and clairvoyant investigation agree—will do so for the next 2,500 years. This bodhisattva will then become Maitreya Buddha, attaining the same rank as did his predecessor, Gautama Buddha.... It is from Christ that all the bodhisattvas receive what they have to impart to human beings in the course of the ages.... A bodhisattva is a teacher until he becomes Buddha; from then onward he is a *power*, an organizing, life-bestowing *power*.... [And if] it were to be the happy fate of humanity that Jeshu ben Pandira—who was inspired at that time by the great bodhisattva, the future Maitreya Buddha—should incarnate again in our epoch, he would consider the task of supreme importance to be that of pointing to the Etheric Christ in the etheric world; and he would emphasize that the Christ came once, and once only, in a physical body. Let us suppose that Jeshu ben Pandira, who was stoned to death approximately one hundred and five years before the Christ Event in Palestine, were to reincarnate in our time and announce the imminence of a revelation of Christ. He would point to the Christ who cannot appear in a physical body but is to become manifest in an etheric form, as he was revealed to Paul at Damascus. By this very teaching Jeshu ben Pandira could be recognized, assuming him to be reincarnated.... [However] it is quite true that a reincarnation of the greatest possible significance might take place in our epoch and be unrecognized or treated with indifference.... If we are resolved to shape our lives in accordance with the living spirit of a new bodhisattva, not with the spirit of a tradition concerning a bodhisattva of the past, then we must make ourselves receptive to the inspiration of the bodhisattva who will subsequently become the Maitreya Buddha. And this bodhisattva will inspire us by drawing attention to the near approach of the time when in a new raiment, in an *etheric* body, Christ will bring life and blessing to those who unfold the new faculties through a new Essene wisdom. We shall speak entirely in the sense of the inspiring bodhisattva who is to become the Maitreya

Buddha.... With the knowledge gained from the inspiration of the bodhisattva himself we declare what form the future manifestation of Christ will take.[11]

Rudolf Steiner spoke several times of Jeshu ben Pandira, the teacher of the Essenes, known also as the Teacher of Righteousness, as an incarnation of the bodhisattva who will become the Maitreya Buddha—an important source being the collection of lectures published with the title: *Esoteric Christianity and the Mission of Christian Rosenkreutz.* The following passages include some indications from these lectures—[3] translated into English by Dorothy Osmond, and [4] translated into English by Robert Powell:

[3] At the present time, words cannot have a direct moral effect. The larynx as it is now would not be capable of uttering such words. But one day this spiritual power will be in existence. Words able to imbue a human being with moral strength will be spoken. Three thousand years from now, the bodhisattva referred to will become Buddha,[12] and his teachings then will cause impulses to stream directly into humanity. He will be the one foreseen by human beings of ancient times: the Maitreya Buddha, bringer of the Good. His mission is to prepare human beings in such a way that they will understand the true nature of the Christ Impulse, to direct their attention more and more intensely upon what they can love, to teach them to transform theory into moral reality, so that finally every thought is integrated into the moral life....

This development is achieved as a prototype by the individuality who assumed the office of bodhisattva when the

---

11   Steiner, *According to Matthew*, lectures 5 and 10 (the quotations cited are from an earlier translation by D. Osmond and M. Kirkcaldy, *The Gospel of St. Matthew*).

12   As described in chapter 1 of this book, the time of the Maitreya Buddha will be in less than 2,500 years from now, around the year 4443, at the transition from the Age of Aquarius to the Age of Capricorn, which will begin in the year 4535. In other lectures (see [2] above) Steiner says 2,500 years (rather than three thousand years from now), 2,500 years being a more accurate indication.

previous bodhisattva, Gautama, became a Buddha. Since then [this individuality] has incarnated once nearly every hundred years. He lived about 100 BC as Jeshu ben Pandira, the herald of Christ. He needs five thousand years to attain the lofty stage of buddhahood, as the Maitreya Buddha. He will be a "bringer of the Good," because—as can be seen by those who are sufficiently clairvoyant—by dint of intense self-discipline one succeeds in developing to a supreme degree powers that cause moral force, magical force, to stream from one, so that through the word itself one will be able to instill right feeling and morality into the souls of human beings. [However] even he who will be the Maitreya Buddha could not yet utter words possessing this magical power. Today it is only *thought* that can be transmitted through the word.... The bodhisattva is preparing for his mission by unfolding in himself to the highest possible stage of development the qualities of serenity and resignation in the face of destiny, attentiveness to events in the surrounding world, selfless devotion, and insight....

In the case of this bodhisattva, a particular law applies. We shall understand this law by remembering the possibility that a complete transformation may take place in the life of the soul at a certain age in life. The greatest of all such transformations came about at the Baptism by John [the Baptist] in the [River] Jordan.... A somewhat similar transformation will take place in him who will become the Maitreya Buddha.... It will always be noticed that, between his thirtieth and thirty-third years, a tremendous change takes place in his life. There will be an exchange of souls, although not to such a complete degree as in the case of Christ. The "I" that dwelled in the body until then passes out of it at this time and the bodhisattva becomes an altogether changed being—although the "I" does not cease to function and is not actually replaced by a different "I" as in the case of Christ Jesus.... What happens is this: the first "I" passes out and a different "I" enters. This may be an individuality such as Moses, or Abraham, or Elijah. This individuality will then be active for a time in the body, thus bringing about the preparation necessary for the Maitreya Buddha.

The bodhisattva lives on for the rest of his life with the "I" that entered into him at that time.... When in some three thousand years from now he becomes the Maitreya Buddha, his "I" will remain in him but will be woven through by another individuality. And this will happen in his thirty-third year, the year when the Mystery of Golgotha was fulfilled by Christ. The Maitreya Buddha will then come forward as the Teacher of the Good, as the mighty Teacher who will transmit the true knowledge and the true wisdom concerning Christ....

The purpose of spiritual science is to make preparation for what will one day take root on the Earth.... I must feel myself to be a link in a chain stretching from the beginning to the end of that process of evolution in which all human beings, all individualities, bodhisattvas, buddhas, and Christ himself, are embraced. I must feel that I am part and parcel of this evolution and so be conscious of the dignity of humanity.[13]

[4] The moment when a bodhisattva becomes a buddha, a new bodhisattva comes. In the moment when Gautama Buddha became Buddha, this bodhisattva individuality was taken from the Earth and a new bodhisattva became active upon the Earth. This bodhisattva will become Buddha at the appointed time. And that time is precisely determined, when the successor of Gautama Buddha, the Maitreya, will become Buddha: five thousand years after Buddha's enlightenment beneath the Bodhi tree. Approximately three thousand years from the present time, the world will experience the incarnation of the Maitreya Buddha, which will be the last incarnation of Jeshu ben Pandira.[14] This bodhisattva, who will come as the Maitreya Buddha, will reincarnate in the flesh, in a physical

---

13   From the two lectures entitled "Jeshu ben Pandira: A Herald of the Christ Impulse" (Leipzig, Nov. 4–5, 1911), containing a wealth of information about the mission of the bodhisattva who will become the Maitreya Buddha. These two lectures, along with others referring to Jeshu ben Pandira, are published in Steiner, *Esoteric Christianity and the Mission of Christian Rosenkreuz.*

14   Concerning the time of 2,500 years until the incarnation of the Maitreya Buddha (actually it will be in less than 2,500 years from now), incarnating around the year 4443, see the comments in [2].

body, also in our century—not, however, as Buddha. It will be his task to give humanity all true concepts concerning the Christ Event....

What is special about the Maitreya Buddha is that he will in a certain sense imitate what took place at the event of Golgotha.... [With him] is given to us the greatest teacher who has appeared in order to reveal to human beings the fullness of the Christ Event. Most remarkable with him will be that, as the greatest teacher, he will bring the most majestic [power of the] word, the highest word.... We are living such that religious longing tends toward Christ. However, the true sources of Christianity have to be found again. *And toward this goal we see flowing together the spiritual stream that proceeds from Jeshu ben Pandira and the one which at the beginning of the thirteenth century connects onto Christian Rosenkreutz.*[15]

[5] Another relevant indication concerning the Maitreya Buddha given by Rudolf Steiner has been translated from the German by Dorothy Lenn and Owen Barfield:

The power of the Christ provides all the impulses to enable human nature to rise again and to see all that has been buried in the depths of the soul—such as for instance, the figures of the Greek gods. That will be the greatest event for the future history of the human soul. It is the event for which spiritual science must prepare, so that the soul may become capable of acquiring etheric vision. In the next three thousand years it will lay hold of more and more souls. The next three thousand years will be devoted to kindling the forces in the human soul which will make it aware of the etheric wonders of Nature around it. It will begin to happen in our own century that one here and one there will see with their etheric souls the reappearing Christ, and within the next three thousand years more and more human beings will see him.

---

15   Translated by R.P. from two lectures referring to Jeshu ben Pandira, published in Steiner, *Esoteric Christianity and the Mission of Christian Rosenkreuz*, lectures 1 and 2 (italics in the final sentence of this quote added by R.P.).

Then will come the fulfillment of the true oriental tradition, a tradition with which all true esotericism is in agreement. At the end of three thousand[16] years the Maitreya Buddha will descend, and will speak to humanity in a form which every human soul will understand, and will mediate the Christ-nature to the human being. That is the secret guarded by oriental mysticism, that about three thousand years after our time the Maitreya Buddha will appear.

What can be added as the contribution of Western culture is that the cosmic Individuality who has *only once* appeared in a human body will become ever more visible to the etheric vision of the human being.... Thereby he will become a trusted friend of the human soul.

Just as two thousand years ago the Buddha spoke of what was natural to the best human souls of his time, so in words which will thrill the soul, the Maitreya Buddha will be able to proclaim everywhere what today cannot be proclaimed publicly: the vision of the Christ in the etheric world which is to come. This is the greatest event of the twentieth century, this upward development of human nature toward what we may call the recurrence of the vision of St. Paul. In the vision at Damascus it came to one person only; in the future it will come little by little to all humanity, beginning in our own century.[17]

We see from this that Steiner spoke on a number of occasions about this particular incarnation—as Jeshu ben Pandira—of the bodhisattva who will become the Maitreya Buddha. However, only on one occasion did he refer to Kashyapa, who was incarnated at the time of Gautama Buddha and was designated by Gautama as his successor in the office of bodhisattva, as described in the following passage:

According to a classic text of Zen Buddhism—*The Transmission of the Light (Denkoroku)*—one day the Buddha

---

16   See [2], where it is indicated that this period is actually 2,500 years.

17   Steiner, *Wonders of the World*, lecture 2, Aug. 19, 1911.

silently raised a lotus blossom and blinked his eyes. At this, Kashyapa smiled. The Buddha said, "I have the treasury of the eye of truth, the ineffable mind of Nirvana. These I entrust to Kashyapa." He also passed his gold brocade robe to Kashyapa, thus indicating Kashyapa to be his successor in the bodhisattva transmission—i.e., the bodhisattva who will become the next Buddha, the future Maitreya Buddha.[18]

The reference by Steiner to Kashyapa is in the context of two lectures, "The Spiritual Bells of Easter," April 10 and 11, 1909, in Cologne. The lectures belong to the first in which Steiner spoke of Christ's return, his Second Coming, in a non-physical form. In these two lectures, Steiner indicates that human beings will behold Christ in spiritual fire, and he refers many times to Kashyapa in relation to the Maitreya Buddha, without speaking out directly that Kashyapa was the bodhisattva who will become the Maitreya Buddha. This fact is *implicit* in these two lectures, but is not stated explicitly. Because of the significance of these two lectures (the only lectures in which Steiner refers to Kashyapa), they are quoted extensively here (translated from the German by Dorothy Osmond & Charles Davy):

[6] Shakyamuni [Gautama Buddha] had a great pupil, and whereas the other pupils grasped to a greater or lesser extent the all-embracing wisdom taught by the Buddha, *Kashyapa*— such was the name of the pupil—grasped it fully. He was one of those most deeply initiated into these teachings, one of the most significant followers of the Buddha. The legend tells that when Kashyapa came to the point of death and because of his mature wisdom was ready to pass into Nirvana, he made his way to a steep mountain and hid himself in a cave. After his death his body did not decay but remained intact.

Only the initiates know of this secret and of the hidden place where the incorruptible body of the great initiate rests. But the Buddha foretold that one day in the future his

---

18   Compare with http://www.ese-an.org/d/218-denko-roku.html.

great successor, the Maitreya Buddha, the new great teacher and leader of humankind, would come, and reaching the supreme height of existence to be attained during earthly life, would seek out the cave of Kashyapa and touch with his right hand the incorruptible body of the Enlightened One. Whereupon a miraculous fire would stream down from heaven and in this fire the incorruptible body of Kashyapa, the Enlightened One, would be lifted from earthly into spiritual existence.

Such is the great Eastern legend—perhaps unintelligible in some respects to the West. This legend speaks, too, of a resurrection, of transportation from earthly existence, an overcoming of death, achieved in such a way that the earth's forces of corruption have no effect upon the purified body of Kashyapa. Thus when the great initiate comes and touches this body with his hand, it will be carried up by the miraculous fire into the heavenly spheres.

It is just where this legend deviates from the content of the Western, Christian account of Easter, that there lies the possibility of reaching a deeper understanding of the Easter festival. Such a legend enshrines an ancient wisdom that can only gradually be approached. We may ask: Why does not Kashyapa, like the Redeemer in the Christian account of Easter, achieve victory over death after three days? Why does the incorruptible body of the Eastern initiate wait for long ages before being transported by the miraculous fire into the heavenly heights?

The human being's breath can be spiritualized through the impulse given by the Mystery of Golgotha—this is the redemption that is achieved by what now lives within us. All the avatars have brought redemption to humanity through power from above, through what has streamed down through them from spiritual heights to the earth. However, the Christ Avatar[19] has redeemed humankind through what he gathered out of the forces of humanity itself, and he has shown us how the forces of redemption, the forces whereby the Spirit becomes victor over matter, can be found *in ourselves*.

---

19   See note by Robert Powell on page 120–121.

Thus, although through the spiritualization of his breath he had made his body incorruptible, even Kashyapa with his supreme enlightenment could not yet find complete redemption. The incorruptible body must wait in the secret cave until it is drawn forth by the Maitreya Buddha. Only when the "I" has spiritualized the physical body to such a degree that the Christ Impulse streams into the physical body is the miraculous *cosmic* fire no longer needed for redemption; for redemption is now brought about by the fire quickened within one's own inner being, in the blood. Thus the radiance streaming from the Mystery of Golgotha is also able to shed light on a legend as wonderful and profound as that of Kashyapa....

We will think once again of the Easter legend which gave us an inkling yesterday of its bearing on this riddle, the legend of Kashyapa, the great sage and enlightened pupil of Shakyamuni. With a vast range of vision and after stupendous endeavors, Kashyapa had absorbed all the wisdom of the East, and it was rightly said of him that of those who came after him no one else was capable, even in the remotest degree, of preserving what he had drawn from Shakyamuni's deep fount of wisdom and—as the last possessor of this primal wisdom—had bestowed upon humankind.

The legend, you will remember, goes on to say that when Kashyapa was on the point of death and felt his entry into Nirvana approaching, he went into a cave in a mountain. There he died in full consciousness, and his body remained immune from decay, hidden from outer humanity and discoverable only by those who through initiation were able to fathom such secrets. It rested uncorrupted in a cave, mysteriously concealed. Furthermore, it was predicted that a great proclaimer of the primeval wisdom in a new form, the Maitreya Buddha, will appear, and having reached the supreme height of his earthly existence, will go to the cave where rests the corpse of Kashyapa. With his right hand he will touch the corpse, and a miraculous fire coming down from the universe will transport the uncorrupted body of Kashyapa into the spiritual worlds.

The Oriental who understands this wisdom waits for the Maitreya Buddha to appear and perform his deed on the uncorrupted body of Kashyapa. Will these two events come about? Will the Maitreya Buddha appear? Will the uncorrupted remains of Kashyapa then be transported by the miraculous fire from heaven? With true Easter feelings we shall be able to glimpse the profound wisdom contained in this legend if we try to understand the nature of the miraculous fire into which the remains of Kashyapa are to be received.

In the previous lecture we saw... that it was the *Christ* who proclaimed himself to Moses in the burning thorn-bush and in thunder and lightning on Sinai; that it was the Christ and no other power than he who declared to Moses: "I am the I AM." Out of the lightning on Sinai he gave the Ten Commandments as a preparation for his coming. Later, he appeared in microcosmic form in Palestine.

In the fire in our blood lives the same God who had announced himself in the heavenly fire and who then, in the Mystery of Palestine, incarnated in a human body in order that his power might permeate the blood where the human fire has its seat. And if we follow the consequences of this event and what it signifies for earth-existence, we shall be able to find the flaming fire into which the remains of Kashyapa will be received....

When was this fire seen again? It was seen again when the eyes of Saul, illumined by clairvoyance on the road to Damascus, beheld and recognized in the radiance of heavenly fire the one who had fulfilled the Mystery of Golgotha. And so both Moses and Paul beheld the Christ: Moses beheld him in the material fire in the burning thorn-bush and in the lightning on Sinai, but only inwardly could he be made aware that it was the Christ who spoke with him. To the enlightened eyes of Paul, Christ revealed himself from the *spiritualized* fire....

It was with grief and profound sorrow that the Eastern sages looked into the future, concerning which they knew that the Maitreya Buddha will one day appear in order to renew the primal wisdom, but that no disciple will be capable of retaining this wisdom. "If the world continues along this course," they said, "the Maitreya Buddha will preach to deaf ears; he will not be understood by human beings wholly engulfed in matter. Moreover, the materiality prevailing on the earth will cause the body of Kashyapa to wither away so that the Maitreya Buddha will not be able to bear his remains into divine-spiritual heights."

It was those with the deepest understanding of Eastern wisdom who looked with such sorrow into the future, wondering whether the earth would be capable of receiving the coming Maitreya Buddha with greater understanding and discernment.

It was necessary that a powerful heavenly force should stream into physical matter, and in physical matter should sacrifice itself. This could not be accomplished by a god merely within the mask of a human form; it had to be accomplished by a human being in the real sense—with human forces, who bore the God within. The Mystery of Golgotha had to take place in order that the matter into which humanity has descended should be made fit, cleansed, purified, and hallowed in such a way as to enable the primal wisdom again to be understood. Humanity today must be brought to realize what the Mystery of Golgotha actually effected in this respect. What then was the real significance of the Event of Golgotha for humankind? How deeply did it penetrate into the human being's whole nature and existence?...

It is indeed true that as the Christ was revealed in advance to Moses and to those who were with him, in the material fire of the thorn-bush and of the lightning on Sinai, so he will be revealed to us in a spiritualized fire of the future. *He is with us always, until the end of the world*, and he will appear in the spiritual fire to those who have allowed their eyes to be enlightened through the Event of Golgotha. Human beings will behold him in *spiritual* fire. They beheld him, to begin with, in a different form; they will behold him for the first time in his true form, in a spiritual fire.

But because the Christ penetrated so deeply into earth-existence—right into the physical bony structure—the power which built his sheaths out of the elements of the earth so purified and hallowed this physical substance that it can never become what in their sorrow the Eastern sages feared: that the Enlightened One of the future, the Maitreya Buddha, would not find on the earth human beings capable of understanding him because they had sunk so deeply into matter. Christ was led to Golgotha in order that he might lift matter again to spiritual heights, in order that the fire might not be extinguished in matter, but be spiritualized. The primal wisdom will again be intelligible to human beings when they themselves are spiritualized—the primal wisdom which, in the spiritual world, was the source of their being. And so the Maitreya Buddha will find understanding on the earth—which would not otherwise have been possible—when human beings have attained deeper insight. We understand far better what we learnt in our youth, when tests in life have matured us, and we can look back upon it all at a later time. Humankind will understand the primal wisdom through being able to look back upon it in the Christ-light streaming from the event of Golgotha.

And now—how can the uncorrupted remains of Kashyapa be rescued, and whither will they be transported? It was said: the Maitreya Buddha will appear, touch these remains with his right hand, and the corpse will be transported in fire. In the fire made manifest to Paul on the road to Damascus we have to see the miraculous, *spiritualized* fire in which the body of Kashyapa will be enshrined. This fire will rescue for future times all that was great and noble in the past. In the spiritualized fire in which Christ appeared to Paul, the body of Kashyapa, untouched by corruption, will be saved through the Maitreya Buddha. Thus we shall see the greatness, the splendor and the wisdom of all the past stream into what humanity has become through the Event of Golgotha....

In the purified spirituality that has poured over the earth and into humankind through the Mystery of Golgotha, everything that has existed in the past is rescued, purified, sustained: just as one day, when the Maitreya Buddha appears, the uncorrupted body of Kashyapa, the great sage of the East, will be purified in the miraculous fire, in the Christ-light which was revealed to Paul on the road to Damascus.[20]

---

20   Steiner, *The Festivals and their Meaning*, "Easter," April 10 and 11, 1909.

Against this background—this being, however, only an *implicit* indication given by Rudolf Steiner—it emerges that prior to the incarnation as Jeshu ben Pandira, the bodhisattva who will become the Maitreya Buddha was incarnated as Kashyapa, the Enlightened One. In chapter one a still earlier incarnation of this bodhisattva is brought into consideration, again based upon an *implicit* indication given by Rudolf Steiner.

In chapter one the significance of the year 2014 in connection with this bodhisattva (Kashyapa/Jeshu ben Pandira/Maitreya) is discussed—the basis for this discussion being the six-hundred year cultural wave spoken of by Rudolf Steiner, with the year 2014 being six hundred years after the start of the fifth cultural epoch in the year 1414.[21] The year 2014, as described in chapter one, also emerges through an ancient prophecy relating to the coming of the Kalki Avatar. Against the background of the identity of the Kalki Avatar with the Maitreya Buddha, this prophecy dovetails in a remarkable way with Steiner's indications given in his lecture of March 13, 1911, published as lecture 9 in the lecture cycle *Background to the Gospel of St. Mark* (translated into English by E.H. Goddard & D.S. Osmond). Steiner speaks concerning the

(7) "side stream that flowed into the direct Christ Impulse at the beginning of a new six-hundred-year period [which] can therefore be described...as a revival of Buddhism.... At the

---

21 The start of the fifth cultural epoch is always given by Steiner as 1413, which he assumed was 2,160 years after the beginning of the fourth cultural epoch, the Greco-Roman epoch, in the year 747 BC, The date of the founding of the city of Rome. Clearly, 747 + 1413 = 2160. However, the date identified by historians as 747 BC is written as -746 by astronomers. Why? This is because historians have no year 0; instead, historians count 3 BC, 2 BC, 1 BC, AD 1, AD 2, AD 3, etc. Since, for computational purposes, a year 0 is necessary, astronomers equate 1 BC with the year 0; 2 BC with -1; 3 BC with -2; etc., signifying that 747 BC = -746. Adding -746 to 2,160 yields 1414. In other words, if the fourth cultural epoch began in 747 BC (this was Steiner's starting point for determining the dating of the cultural epochs), then it follows that the starting date of the fifth cultural epoch was the year 1414. Adding six hundred years to 1414, we arrive at the year 2014.

present time a renewed influx of the Buddha stream is taking place. If we are able to see these things in the right light, it will become evident that we have to absorb the elements of the Buddha stream that were not hitherto present in Western culture. And we can see how certain elements of the Buddha stream are actually making their way into the spiritual development of the West; for instance, the teaching of reincarnation and karma....

There is Buddhism that has progressed to further stages of development.... We contemplate the Buddha at the further stage of his development in the realm of the spirit, who proclaims from there the truths of basic importance for our time.... According to the Eastern legend Buddha passed into Nirvana, having handed on the bodhisattva's crown to his successor, who is now a bodhisattva and will subsequently become the Maitreya Buddha of the future.... In hidden worlds the union has meanwhile taken place between Buddhism and Christianity.... If we trace the course of Buddhism as an enduring stream...we can accept it only in the changed form in which it now appears. If through clairvoyant insight we understand the inspirations of the Buddha, we must speak to him as he actually exists today."[22]

Steiner's indication concerning a "revival of Buddhism" flowing into the "direct Christ Impulse" is strengthened by the prophecy discussed in chapter one concerning the coming of the bodhisattva who will become the Maitreya Buddha/Kalki Avatar—this prophecy relating to the year 2014. Since this bodhisattva is the direct successor of Gautama Buddha, what better individuality to help spearhead a revival of Buddhism? If the ancient prophecy is accurate, the Kalki–Maitreya individuality should emerge in the year 2014 and begin to unfold a mighty spiritual impulse in which Buddha and Christ work together, side by side. In chapter one this is explored against the background of the current world situation, where an impulse for the Good is sorely needed. Since Christ is

---

22 Steiner, *Background to the Gospel of St. Mark*, lecture 9, Mar. 13, 1911.

the Good, and since Maitreya means "bearer of the Good," it is clear that there is a close relationship between the Maitreya Bodhisattva and Christ. The Maitreya comes with a two-edged sword, for the Good and against evil.

Evil prefers to work in darkness, in secrecy. And one of the ways of combating evil is to bring the working of evil to the light of day. Hence the importance of the fact that in June and July 2013 the evil plan for establishing a global surveillance state was brought to the light of day. As Joseph Pulitzer said, "There is not a crime, there is not a dodge, there is not a trick, there is not a swindle, there is not a vice, which does not live by secrecy."[23]

> Our Republic and its press will rise or fall together. An able, disinterested, public-spirited press, with trained intelligence to know the right and courage to do it, can preserve that public virtue without which popular government is a sham and a mockery. A cynical, mercenary, demagogic press will produce in time a people as base as itself. The power to mould the future of the Republic will be in the hands of the journalists of future generations.[24]

We can learn from the examples of history. Both Nazi Germany and the Soviet Union implemented spying programs to spy on their peoples. However, their governments did not have access to the highly sophisticated surveillance technology which exists now. It is only now, by way of this new surveillance technology, that the possibility exists for establishing a global surveillance state. It remains to be seen whether the drive to establish a global surveillance state will continue now that it has been exposed, or whether the peoples of the world will acquiesce to the most advanced spying system—one that is far more sophisticated than those of Nazi Germany and the Soviet Union—in

---

23   See http://www.goodreads.com/quotes/239097-there-is-not-a-crime
     -there-is-not-a-dodge.

24   See http://www.goodreads.com/quotes/4180-our-republic-and-its-press
     -will-rise-or-fall-together.

the history of humankind. Humanity stands at an important threshold for the future, where the choice is between freedom and control. For, as the spying programs of Nazi Germany and the Soviet Union revealed, they were about controlling the people. Now that we have advanced beyond these totalitarian states, in the spirit of democracy should there not be a public debate and a poll asking each citizen—each citizen who is entitled to vote—this question:

Answer "yes" or "no"—Do you want to be spied on by the government?

The bodhisattva who will become the Maitreya Buddha, like Rudolf Steiner before him, is a fighter for human freedom, and is thus an important ally in the great struggle now taking place in the world. For freedom is the foundation for the development of love. And the goal of human evolution is the unfolding of humanity's future calling as spirits of freedom and love. Both Rudolf Steiner and the Maitreya are messengers of Christ, who holds the vision of the plan of evolution leading toward humanity becoming the spiritual hierarchy of freedom and love[25] and whose activity in the etheric realm—which we are free to unite with or not—is to lead us toward the realization of the evolutionary plan.

This breath of freedom and love weaves through the texts of visions of the Maitreya received by the seer Estelle Isaacson, which are included in this book with a view to helping the reader to draw inwardly nearer to this "greatest teacher" whose mission it is "to reveal to human beings the fullness of the Christ Event" (Steiner's words, quoted in citation [4]). It is the presence of Christ in the etheric realm to which the Maitreya seeks to align us, if we choose, in freedom, to take the path of aligning ourselves with Christ. This path is the answer to the

---

25 Steiner, *The Spiritual Hierarchies and the Physical World*, lecture 10, Apr. 18, 1909: "Humanity will be the hierarchy of freedom and love."

"destructive programs of the evil one"—Estelle Isaacson's words from her vision "Align with Me and Think Good Thoughts." The drive toward establishing a global surveillance state is one example of these "destructive programs of the evil one." As she describes, further:

> By thinking thoughts of the Good, one does the work of the Maitreya, who will be able to take those Good thoughts and bring forth the Good on Earth. He will bring to pass the physical manifestation of the spiritual creations now underway by those beings who are thinking Good thoughts.
>
> > Blessed are those who can think the thoughts
> > of the angelic realm.
> > Blessed are those who are invited to work
> > with the Maitreya.

❀

Finally, a word about seership: Steiner speaks of the "sublime gift of seership," by which he means, of course, the new, authentic, Christ-inspired seership, inspired by the Etheric Christ. For the full context of these words about the sublime gift of seership, see further on for Steiner's words spoken by the seer Theodora from his first mystery drama. While I cannot warrant Estelle Isaacson's visions as being accurate in every detail, I have through years of personal acquaintance with Estelle and her visions gained increasing confidence in their overall accuracy, appropriateness, and moral depth. Her visions are, I believe, an example of the new, authentic, Christ-inspired seership exemplified by the figure of Theodora in Rudolf Steiner's first mystery play. Nevertheless, this does not obviate the necessity for each reader to carefully examine the content of this book in a discerning way. In this age of freedom it is of paramount importance that individuals decide for themselves concerning the truth—or lack of truth—of statements made by others.

The vision of Christ's Second Coming as seen by the seer, Theodora—from the first scene of Rudolf Steiner's first mystery play, *The Portal of Initiation*:

I am compelled to speak. Before my soul
Appears a light-filled image,
Whose words resound within me.
I feel myself in future times,
And human beings do I behold as yet unborn.
They also see the image; they, too,
Can hear the words, which thus resound:
"O you who lived in faith, comforted by hope,
Take comfort now in beholding, and
Receive new life through Me. For I am He
Who lived in the souls of those who sought Me within—
Through the words of My messengers,
Through contemplative forces of heart and mind.
You saw the light of the sensory realm and had to believe
In the creative spirit-world beyond.
Now, however, you have yourselves achieved
A taste of the sublime gift of seership.
O feel it in your souls."

Emerging from that radiant light,
A human figure speaks to me:
"Thou shalt make known to all who have ears to hear
That thou hast seen
What human beings shall experience one day.
Christ once lived upon the earth,
And resulting from this life it ensued
That in soul form He weaves o'er
The evolution of humankind.
He united with the earth's own spirit-sphere.
When manifesting in such forms of existence,
He was not yet visible to human beings,
Because they lacked the spiritual eyes
That will emerge in future times.
Yet even now this future is at hand,

When human beings on earth
Shall be gifted with new seership.
What once the senses saw, when Christ lived
Upon the earth, shall be seen by souls,
As the time of fulfillment is near."[26]

---

26 Steiner, *Four Mystery Plays,* "The Portal of Initiation," scene 1
(translation of Theodora's words revised by R.P.).

Appendix 2:

Valentin Tomberg on the Coming Buddha-Avatar, Maitreya-Kalki

In chapter 1, some quotations by Valentin Tomberg regarding the bodhisattva who will become the Maitreya Buddha were discussed. The following material is composed of other, supplementary material by Valentin Tomberg on this theme:

(1) When it comes to understanding ideas, the point is not to spin them into a system of logic, but to root them firmly in the spiritual moral organism of Christ's cosmic work. In the Apocalypse, such work is called the "name of Christ," and "not denying" his "name" is the soul attitude that accepts as true only ideas indebted not just to logic, but also always to the moral forces. Not to deny the "name" is moral logic, just as amoral, formal knowledge is itself a denial of the name of Christ, since it excludes the voice of goodness from the realm of knowing. The faculty of the *word* and that of *moral logic* (keeping the word and not denying the name) will be most highly developed at the beginning of the sixth epoch, that of Philadelphia [Revelation 3:7], when the Maitreya Buddha, the "Bringer of Goodness," will appear. The special task of the Maitreya is to develop what has "little strength"—the *word* and the *thought*—into a power that will regain a position in the world that allows a cultural community to evolve. The moral force of the word will live and work so powerfully in the Maitreya that human beings will be stopped and will experience a spiritual conversion...through the magical, moral influence of the word. Thoughts will no longer merely explain the nature of goodness, but actually transmit it. The Maitreya Buddha will not merely show goodness; he will awaken it in the soul. Therefore, the effect of his word, as

a great movement among humankind, will become the foundation of a new culture. This was the effect on those whom Gautama Buddha referred to when he spoke the prophecy concerning the Bodhisattva Maitreya, who would become the next Buddha: "He will be the leader of a band of disciples numbering hundreds of thousands, as I am now the leader of bands of disciples numbering hundreds."[1] From those hundreds of thousands will emerge the power to determine the life forms of the sixth post-Atlantean epoch—life forms that express the new Pentecost experience and the Pentecostal influence of the word.[2]

(2) The Christ concept of the sixth cultural epoch is revealed with these words: "And to the angel of the church in Philadelphia write: These things saith he that is holy, he that is true, he that hath the key of David, he that openeth, and no man shutteth; and shutteth, and no man openeth" [Rev. 3:7]. The Christ being will be experienced most of all as the force that leads to truth and morality (the true and the holy), to be felt and to function as a unity. The Maitreya Buddha of the sixth epoch will reveal exactly the new relationship between the "holy" and the "true," or between morality and logic, which are identical in the Christ being. "Moral logic" arises from an experience of the Christ impulse...the impulse causing knowledge and morality to operate as a unity. It is this unity that "opens the door," bestowing the karmic faculty that makes possible communication with the spiritual world. This karmic capacity based on fidelity to the future is called the "key of David," since David's character answered the manas consciousness.... The Christ of the sixth cultural epoch appears as the initiator who opens the door—that is, as the Greater Guardian of the Threshold, whom the sixth cultural epoch has the purpose of meeting. The Christianity of that period will be characterized especially by the fact that Christ is recognized and experienced under the aspect of the Guardian of the Threshold.[3]

---

1   *Cakkavattisuttanti*, quoted in Oldenberg, *Buddha: His Life, His Doctrine, His Order.*

2   Tomberg, *Christ and Sophia*, p. 345.

3   Ibid., p. 351.

(3) THE REVELATION OF THE MAITREYA BUDDHA IN JESUS CHRIST:

Legend speaks of Buddha handing over his crown, his positive karma, to another, to his successor, the Maitreya Buddha. Both were present at the birth of Christ: the *Nirmanakaya* of the old Buddha, and the Maitreya Buddha, the future Buddha—see, for example, Luke 4:31–44, where healing occurs through the word. [Healing through the word is indicative of the presence of the Maitreya Buddha—Luke 4:31–37, healing of someone possessed; Luke 4:38–39, healing of Peter's mother-in-law; Luke 4:40–44, healing the sick and possessed.] The Maitreya Buddha will not adopt a stance of flight from the world. Rather, he will be the *Maitreya*—i.e., effecting good *in* the world. The Maitreya Buddha works in Jesus through the word and through healings. Thus, healings take place through the coming about of changes in the [human] organism through him. He does not content himself with singing about the positive, like Francis of Assisi, but he also judges over evil—see Luke 11:39–43 ["woe to the Pharisees"]. He fights against the demons. Buddha wanted solely to bring the good. The Maitreya Buddha, however, also fights against evil. He had a two-edged sword: for the good and against evil.

The Maitreya Buddha Stream in the World (the Foundation Stone Meditation)

Where does the working of the Maitreya Buddha already come to expression? The Christmas Foundation Meeting [of the Anthroposophical Society] arose through the spirit of the Maitreya Buddha, and the Foundation Stone Meditation [given by Rudolf Steiner], especially the fourth part, where the working of the Maitreya Buddha emerges in the cooperation of head and heart. The Christmas Foundation Meeting should be a preparation for the working of the Maitreya Buddha, who began to work in 1932/33.

The Jupiter Human Being: Revelations 1:12–16

If one succeeds in recognizing and taking up the guidance of the Maitreya Buddha, where would that lead us?—to becoming "Jupiter human beings," [that is] human beings who have already developed their entire Manas [organisation], who have developed the faculty of Imagination. This is what the human being becomes when he learns to create and to work into culture with his [faculty of] Imagination, for example, to heal. [Thus he becomes] a complete Manas human being. In the Book of Revelations, the Manas human being is described thus[4]: "One like a Son of Man, clothed with a long robe down to his feet (turning the will outward as a kind of enveloping sheath) and with a golden girdle around his breast (the form-giving and constricting force of the head [having] descended into the Sun-region of the heart); his head and his hair were white as white wool, white as snow (thinking, having become cosmic, becomes white); as also his eyes were like flames of fire (seeing will then be a radiation that illumines and penetrates, coming from within, the appearances of the external world); his feet were like burnished bronze (earth on Jupiter), refined as in a furnace; and his voice was like the sound of many waters (the driving, creative force of Nature); in his right hand he held seven stars; from his mouth issued a sharp two-edged sword (the magic of the word); and his face was like the Sun shining in full strength (the extended Sun forces of the heart become raised to the head).[5]

---

4 This description is an abbreviated version of that from Tomberg, *Christ and Sophia*, pp. 317–318.

5 (3) is from the unpublished *Lord's Prayer Course*, weeks 20–22, by Valentin Tomberg, available as a study course, in installments, from the Sophia Foundation (www.sophiafoundation.org), translated by Robert Powell from Valentin Tomberg's German notes (words in brackets [ ] added by R.P.). Note that "unpublished" refers to the English translation. A German edition has been published in four volumes: *Der Vaterunser-Kurs* (Taisersdorf, Germany: Achamoth Verlag, 2008–2010).

(4) WHAT IS THE NATURE OF BUDDHAHOOD?

Human goodness—what the human being has as content of herself [himself] in the will: goodness becomes humanized. The purified and controlled astral body of the Buddha is behind this. ("The body that [such a being as Buddha] assumes after attaining enlightenment [having passed through the stage of perfection] and in which he can work down upon the earth from above in the way described, this body is called a *Nirmanakaya*. We can therefore say that the *Nirmanakaya* of Buddha appeared to the shepherds [near Bethlehem] in the form of the angelic hosts. Buddha appeared in the radiance of his *Nirmanakaya*." [6])

Buddha reached peace [through control] of the astral body. He allowed [this] peace to flow into the world. He brought meekness into the world. Behind this, however, stood the ideal of *Nirvana*, eternal peace. Non-participatory [detached] beholding. This is actually the gaze of the recently departed [deceased]. After [the proclamation of Buddha to the shepherds in his *Nirmanakaya* resulting in] his connection with the Nathan Jesus, his condition changed. Now meekness has become active, carrying over to the other beings—an active mildness (Francis of Assisi). Earlier, Buddha did not destroy and did not kill. It was only later, however, that warmth and compassion entered his gaze in beholding. His student, *Ananda*, is someone who would never kill a wolf. However, St. Francis tamed the wolf and named it "Brother Wolf." This is [here is revealed] the step to Christian meekness. Buddha is also an office [position]. [There exists] an unbroken line of buddhahood, which always has the task of transmitting meekness. [Here] the Maitreya Buddha [the next Buddha] represents progress [to the next step]: the metamorphosis of meekness. In the first chapter of the Gospel of Luke there is much concerning Buddha and concerning the Maitreya. The formula *Glory to God* [in the heights and peace on earth to all beings

---

6   Steiner, *According to Luke*, p. 77 (translation edited by R.P.).

of good will] is elaborated upon in the Foundation Stone meditation [given by Rudolf Steiner on December 25, 1923; see appendix 3]. [It is a matter of] regulating thinking-feeling-will as it corresponds to the level of meekness of the Maitreya Buddha:

1st verse: stream from above → below ↓

2nd verse: stream in the horizontal → left/right →

3rd verse: stream from below → above ↑

4th verse: stream from Christ → Jesus +

What is new here is that it is spoken out by the human being. He, the Maitreya Buddha, will bring magical power to the human word, whereby human beings [will] come to meekness. Thus, we [will] come to the creation of meekness. And the figure of the Jupiter human being of [chapter 1 of] the Apocalypse is a human being who has developed meekness. He is a human being creating Imaginations. We see here how the figure [of the Jupiter human being] has completely become activity. [In this case] all Imagination has become [magically creative by way of] magical signs and deeds. This is the ideal of buddhahood. And such a human being has already inherited the earth.[7]

(5) The great spiritual work—seen always on the historical plane—takes place under simultaneous action stemming from two contrasting sources: from above and from below—i.e., under the action of continuous revelation and that of the effort of human consciousness. In other words, it is the product of the collaboration of revelation and humanism, or of avatars and buddhas—to say it in terms of the Indo-Tibetan spiritual tradition. This latter awaits both a new wave of revelation, the culminating point of which will be the Kalki Avatar, and the manifestation of a new Buddha—the Maitreya Buddha. At the same time esoteric Islam *(batin)*—Shi'ism and Sufism—awaits the coming *(parousia)* of the twelfth imam

---

7   Tomberg, *Lord's Prayer Course/Our Mother Course*, weeks 538–539 (translated by R.P.; available as a correspondence course from the Sophia Foundation, www.sophiafoundation.org).

"who, at the end of our era, will bring the full revelation of the esotericism of all divine revelations" (Henri Corbin, *Histoire de la philosophie islamique,* Paris, 1964, p. 21), and believing Jews await the coming of the Messiah. We need hardly mention, also, the widespread expectation of the Second Coming of Christ.

Thus, there is a climate of expectation in the world—expectation sustained, contemplated and intensified through the course of the centuries. Without being nourished and directed from above, this energy of human expectation alone would have exhausted itself long ago. But it is not exhausted; rather, on the contrary, it is growing. This is because it aspires to a reality and not an illusion. And this reality is the historical accomplishment of the great work of uniting spirituality and intellectuality, revelation and humanism, on the vast scale of the whole of humankind.

Seen on the level of the history of the whole of humankind, this work presents itself as follows:

We mentioned above the oriental notions of avatars and imams, on the one hand, and that of buddhas, on the other hand. Avatars and imams represent personalities who are culminating points of the revelation from above, while buddhas (Gautama Buddha being only one in a series of buddhas) represent the culminating points of certain epochs of human history—not of revelation from above, but rather of the awakening of human consciousness. The word *buddha* signifies "awakened," whereas that of *avatar* signifies "descent"—"a descent, the birth of God in humanity, the Godhead manifesting itself in the human form and nature (this is) the eternal avatar" (Sri Aurobindo Ghose, *Essays on the Gita,* Madras, 1922, p. 190). Therefore, if avatars are *descents* of the divine, buddhas *are ascents* of the human—they are culminating points of stages of *humanism* in the process of evolution. The difference between the "revelatory ones" (avatars and imams) and the "awakened ones" (buddhas) is analogous to that between "saints" and "righteous individuals" in the Judeo-Christian world.

Here "saints" correspond to avatars in that they represent the revelation of divine grace through them and in them, and "righteous men" correspond to buddhas in that they bring to evidence the fruits of human endeavor.

Thus, Job was not a saint, but a righteous man—one of those righteous individuals who "maintain the world" through their merits. Righteous individuals show how great the value is of human nature when its very essence is awakened and revealed. Righteous individuals are the true humanists—the flowers of pure humanism. They bear witness to the fact that the essence of human nature is in the image and likeness of God. This was the witness borne by Job, and it was the witness borne by Socrates. The German philosopher Immanuel Kant bore witness also, by declaring loudly that, however bereft the human soul might be of illuminating grace from above and revelation from above, it bears in itself the *categorical imperative*—immanent moral law (called *dharma* by the sages of India)—which makes it act and think as if it were eternal, immortal, and aspiring to infinite perfection. Thus Kant bore witness to the fundamental nobility of human nature—and this was his contribution *to faith in human beings*, whatever their limitations, and even errors, in the metaphysical domain may be. For just as there are two loves—love of God and love of neighbor—which are inseparable, so there are *two faiths* which are also inseparable—faith in God and faith in humankind. Saints and martyrs bear witness to God and righteous individuals bear witness to the human being as the image and likeness of God. The former restore and strengthen faith in God and the latter restore and strengthen faith in the human being. And it is faith in Jesus Christ, in the God-Human, that unites faith in God and that in the human being, just as love for Jesus Christ unites love of God and love of one's neighbor.

In Jesus Christ we have the perfect union of divine revelation and the most pure humanism. Which means to say that not only all avatars but also all buddhas of the past and of the future are summarized in Jesus Christ—being the Logos made flesh, and his Humanity having realized the most complete awakening of all what is of divine essence in human nature. For Jesus Christ is the revelation that God is love, and he bears witness that the essence of human nature is love. And can one conceive of, can one Imagine, anything more divine than love and anything more human than love? For this reason all avatars (including all prophets and all imams) and all buddhas (including all sages, all initiates and all bodhisattvas) were, are, and will be only degrees and aspects of the divine revelation and the human awakening realized in Jesus Christ.

This truth, evident for everyone whose head and heart are united in thought (i.e., for one who uses *moral logic*), is nevertheless very difficult for those making use of *formal logic*—in the domain of humanity's history or in the domain of philosophy—to understand and accept.

Now, the following words of Krishna in the *Bhagavad Gita* relate to the doctrine of avatars:

> Many births of yours and mine, O Arjuna, have taken place.... Though I am unborn (having no birth), though I am imperishable, though I am master of the elements, yet out of my *maya* (power of illusion) I take birth, resting on (material) Nature. Whensoever, O Bharata, virtue *(adharmasya,* the law of righteousness) languishes and sin predominates, I create myself (I take birth). I take birth age after age, for the liberation of the good and the destruction of the wicked, and for the establishment of piety (true religion).[8]

In commenting on this, Sri Aurobindo says:

> The avatar comes as the manifestation of the divine nature in the human nature, the apocalypse of its Christhood, Krishnahood, buddhahood, in order that the human nature may, by moulding its principle, thought, feeling, action, being

---

8   *Bhagavad Gita,* iv, 5–8; trsl. M. N. Dutt, Bhishma Parva xxviii, 5–8, in *The Mahabharata* VI, p. 37.

on the lines of that Christhood, Krishnahood, buddhahood, transfigure itself into the divine. The law, the Dharma which the avatar establishes is given for that purpose chiefly; the Christ, Krishna, Buddha stands in its centre as the gate, he makes through himself the way men shall follow. That is why each incarnation (avatar) holds before men his own example and declares of himself that he is the way and the gate; he declares, too, the oneness of his humanity with the divine being, declares that the Son of Man and the Father above from whom he has descended are one, that Krishna in the human body... and the supreme Lord and Friend of all creatures are but two revelations of the same divine Purushottama, revealed there in his own being, revealed here in the type of humanity.[9]

Nothing could be clearer and more convincing! Avatars are therefore periodic incarnations of the Divine; they incarnate periodically with a view to reestablishing the law, just like prophets, who arise to the same end, and they are, each time, doors and ways—Sons of God and Sons of Man who are one with their Father in heaven. And Sri Aurobindo concludes:

Nor does it matter essentially in what form and name or putting forward what aspect of the Divine he (the avatar) comes; for in all ways, varying with their nature, men are following the path set to them by the Divine which will in the end lead them to him and the aspect of him which suits their nature is what they can best follow when he comes to lead them; in whatever way men accept, love and take joy in God, in that way God accepts, loves and takes joy in man.[10]

All this appears as the breath of pure reason—the most resolute ecumenism and universal tolerance. But is not this tolerance, this ecumenism and this reasonability of the doctrine of avatars, such as it is professed by Sri Aurobindo, in principle identical with the reasonability, ecumenism and tolerance manifested by the leaders

9   Sri Aurobindo Ghose, *Essays on the Gita*, pp. 190–191.

10   Ibid., p. 226.

of the Roman empire who conceived of the idea of a temple for all the gods—i.e., the Pantheon?—the Pantheon with a place of honor given to Jesus Christ alongside Jupiter, Osiris, Mithras, and Dionysius? For all these gods have this in common, that they are immortal and superior to the human being. And is not Christ immortal, since he resurrected from the dead?—and is he not superior to the human being, as his miracles prove? Therefore, he belongs to the category of gods and has the right to be admitted to their ranks at the Pantheon.

Theoretically there are ten avatars of Vishnu in Hinduism (e.g. Matsyavatara, Varahavatara, Narasimhavatara, Vamanavatara), but Rama and Krishna are the most popular and most celebrated amongst them. With respect to the avatar to come, Kalkin or Kalki, he is spoken of in the *Kalki-Purana* as the avatar who will mark the end of the age of iron; he will be clothed in the form of a giant, with the head of a horse—a symbol which appeals to our faculty of meditative deepening. Sri Aurobindo mentions—and this on many occasions—only Christ, Krishna, and Buddha.

Nevertheless, Buddha (whom, it is true, Hinduism has included in its pantheon, just as Islam sees in Jesus Christ one of the prophets, the last of whom was Mohammed) does not in any way correspond to the fundamental characteristic of avatars given by Sri Aurobindo, namely:

> Each Incarnation (avatar) holds before human beings his own example and declares of himself that he is the way and the gate; he declares too the oneness of his humanity with the divine being...that the Son of Man and the Father above from whom he has descended are one.[11]

It is an incontestable fact that Sakyamuni, the historical Buddha, never declared the identity of his human being with divine being (not to mention that he never declared himself to be one with the Father in heaven). The *Dishanikaya,* a long

---

11   Ibid., p. 191.

collection of Buddha's discourses in Pali, contradicts it on each page and uses a multitude of arguments and facts to the sole end of persuading the reader (or listener to the Buddha's discourses) that Buddha was the *awakened man*—i.e., he became completely conscious of the common and ordinary human experience on earth—that of birth, sickness, old age and death—and drew from it practical and moral conclusions which are summarised in his eightfold path. The point shown by the *Dishanikaya* is that it is not the extraordinary experience of a mystic or gnostic revelation which made the prince of Kapilavastu a Buddha, but rather that he awoke to a new understanding of ordinary human experience—of the human condition as such. It was a man—and not a messenger from heaven—who awoke from the sleep of passive acceptance, habit, the stupefying influence of transitory desires, and the hypnotic force of the totality of human conventions.

The Buddha's teaching is that of a human spirit who took account, in a state of complete lucidity, of the human condition in general and of the practical and moral consequences to be drawn from it. It is an analysis of the reality of human life, and an establishment of the unique consequences which result necessarily from this analysis, by a human spirit five centuries before Jesus Christ, who was placed beyond the Jewish and Iranian prophetic tradition. The Buddha's teaching is therefore humanism pure and simple, which has nothing to do with the revelation from above by prophets and avatars.

It is necessary, therefore, to eliminate Buddha from the three avatars mentioned by Sri Aurobindo: "Christ, Krishna, and Buddha."

Concerning Jesus Christ, he did not come solely "for the liberation of the good and the destruction of the wicked, and for the establishment of the throne of *justice" (Bhagavad Gita* iv, 8), but above all to vanquish evil and death, for the establishment of the throne of love. Jesus Christ was not only a divine *birth* but also, and above all, the divine *death*—i.e., resurrection—which is not the mission of any avatar, of the past or yet to come. The work of Jesus Christ differs from that of avatars in that it signifies the *expiatory sacrifice* for completely fallen humankind. This means to say that human beings—who before Jesus Christ had only the choice between renunciation and affirmation of the world of birth and death—are put in the position, since the mystery of Calvary, of transforming it—the Christian ideal being "a new heaven and a new earth" (Rev. 21:1). The mission of an avatar, however, is "the liberation of the good" in this fallen world, without even attempting to transform it. It is a matter in the work of Jesus Christ of universal salvation—the work of divine magic and divine alchemy, that of the transformation of the fallen world—and not only of the liberation of the good. The work of Jesus Christ is the divine magical operation of love aiming at universal salvation through the transformation of humankind and of Nature.

As well as Buddha, therefore, it is necessary to eliminate Jesus Christ, also, from the abridged list of avatars given by Sri Aurobindo. Thus, only Krishna remains, one who is, in addition to Rama, the avatar *par excellence* of Hinduism.

Although we refute Sri Aurobindo's classification of Buddha and Jesus Christ in the category of avatars, we should do justice to this Indian sage: his idea of Jesus Christ is infinitely more elevated and nearer to the truth than that of self-styled Christian theologians of the so-called "liberal" Protestant school who regard Jesus Christ as a simple carpenter from Nazareth, who taught and lived the moral ideal of love of God and neighbor. Even every muezzin of Cairo or Baghdad has a notion of Jesus Christ that is more just than that of these theologians, since the former regard him as a prophet inspired by God. With respect to Sri Aurobindo, he regards Jesus Christ as a divine incarnation and makes it understood—by always placing Jesus Christ at the head of the other avatars ("Christ, Krishna, Buddha") that he, personally, considers him as a light of the first magnitude in the heaven of divine avatars!

But let us now return to the arcanum of the alchemical work of the fusion of spirituality and intellectuality, as seen on the historical plane.

After Jesus Christ—the God-Human, who was the complete unity not only of spirituality and intellectuality, but also of divine will and human will, and even of divine essence and human essence—the work of the fusion of spirituality and intellectuality can be nothing other than the germination of the Christic seed in human nature and consciousness. In other words, it is a matter of the progress of the *Christianization* of humanity, not only in the sense of a growing number of baptized people, but above all in the sense of a qualitative transformation of human nature and consciousness. This latter will work in conformity with the law: general aspiration and longing; culminating point of success in an individuality; general diffusion spread out over a number of generations—i.e., the climate of general expectation will lead to the particular realization which will subsequently become general. This is why Buddhists await the coming of the Maitreya Buddha and Hindus that of the Kalki Avatar. They await him, having in view a step forward in humanity's spiritual evolution that will be crossed as a consequence of the manifestation of the new Buddha and the new avatar. And this step forward will be nothing other than the fusion of spirituality and intellectuality.

This expectation is, moreover, not restricted to the East:

Theosophists made a considerable contribution to it by launching a movement of international scope aiming at preparing minds for the coming—supposedly at hand—of the new teacher. To this end they founded the Order of the Star of the East which numbered about 250,000 members, and which organized congresses, conferences and rallies all over the place, as well as publishing hundreds of books and brochures. Whilst spreading the idea of the imminent coming of a new teacher for humanity, the Order of the Star of the East was, alas, too fixed on a particular personality chosen not by heaven, but rather by the leaders of the Theosophical Society, who was extolled in advance so as to build up his prestige, which in the last analysis displeased this person, who disbanded the Order.

It was more discreetly, and without putting a particular person in the limelight as candidate, that Dr. Rudolf Steiner, founder of the Anthroposophical Society, predicted the manifestation—again in the first half of the twentieth century—not of the new Maitreya Buddha or Kalki Avatar, but rather of the bodhisattva—i.e., the individuality in the process of becoming the next Buddha, whose field of activity he hoped the Anthroposophical Society would serve. A new disappointment! This time the disappointment was due not to an error with regard to the awaited individuality, nor even with regard to the time of the beginning of his activity, but rather to an overestimation of the Anthroposophical Society on the part of its founder—thus nothing became of it.

Be that as it may, the idea and the expectation of the coming of the new buddha and new avatar lives at present both in the western world and in the orient. There is much confusion concerning this idea, above all among theosophists, but there are also those who see clearly here. Rudolf Steiner, for example, saw very clearly: of all that has been written and said in public, the most correct is what was said by Rudolf Steiner. He was on the right track, at least.

Now, in following the same track—that leading to the culminating point of the fusion of spirituality and intellectuality—we arrive at the following synopsis:

Since it is a question of the work of the fusion of revelation and knowledge, of spirituality and intellectuality, it is a matter throughout of the fusion of the avatar principle with the Buddha principle. In other words, the Kalki Avatar awaited by the Hindus and the Maitreya Buddha awaited by the Buddhists will manifest in a *single personality.* On the historical plane the Maitreya Buddha and the Kalki Avatar will be one.

This means to say that the awaited avatar "with the body of a giant and the head of a horse" (Kalki) and the expected Buddha who will be the "bringer of good" (Maitreya) will be one and the same personality. And this personality will signify the complete union of the most elevated humanism (the principle of the Buddhas) and the highest revelation (the principle of the avatars) of a kind that both the spiritual world and the human world will speak and act simultaneously and hand-in-hand through him. In other words, the Buddha Avatar to come will *not only speak of the good but he will speak the good;* he will not merely teach the way of salvation, but he will advance the course of this way; he will not be solely a witness of the divine and spiritual world, but he will make human beings into authentic witnesses of this world; he will not simply explain the profound meaning of revelation, but he will bring human beings themselves to attain to the illuminating experience of revelation, of a kind that it will not be he who will win authority, but rather He who is "the true light that enlightens every human being entering the world" (John 1, 9)—Jesus Christ, the Word made flesh, who is the way, the truth, and the life. The mission of the Buddha Avatar to come will therefore not be the foundation of a new religion, but rather that of bringing human beings to first-hand experience of the source itself of all revelation ever received from above by humankind, as also of all essential truth ever conceived of by humanity. It will not be novelty to which he will aspire, but rather the conscious certainty of eternal truth.

Maitreya-Kalki, the Buddha Avatar, will represent the fusion of *prayer and meditation,* these two forms of spiritual activity being the motivating forces of spiritual religion and spiritual humanism. The apparent incompatibility of the state of consciousness represented by statues of the master of meditation, Gautama

Buddha, plunged in meditation in the asana posture, and that of St. Francis of Assisi receiving the stigmata whilst kneeling in prayer—this apparent incompatibility, I say—will be surmounted by the Buddha Avatar to come. The fire of prayer will unite with the limpid water of the peace of meditation; the alchemical marriage of the sun and moon, of fire and water, will take place in him.

The union of the principles of prayer and meditation which the future Buddha Avatar will represent will be, in fact, the crowning of a long series of efforts aiming at this end through the course of the centuries—the result of a long preparation through the course of humankind's spiritual history. For not only was prayer introduced into the strictly meditative Indo-Tibetan Mahayana school of Buddhism—under the form of Lamaism—and into Hinduism under the form of Bhakti yoga, but also meditation was introduced to the West in the guise of complementing and helping the life of prayer in the spiritual practice of the great religious orders. St. Bonaventura, for example, introduced it into the Franciscan Order, St. Teresa and St. John of the Cross introduced it into the Carmelite Order, and St. Ignatius of Loyola, the founder of the Jesuit Order, was a master not only of prayer but also of meditation. One could say that this latter to a large extent prefigured the fusion of spirituality and intellectuality, of prayer and meditation, which is the mission of the future Buddha Avatar. The *calm warmth* of complete certainty, due to the cooperation of human effort and revelation from above, which St. Ignatius possessed and which his disciples (of his spiritual exercises) attained where meditation and prayer are united—make an impressive prefiguring of the Buddha Avatar to come.[12]

∞

Note by R.P.: The foregoing analysis concerning buddhas and avatars seems not only to contradict but also to refute Sri Aurobindo's exposition

---

12   Anonymous, *Meditations on the Tarot*, pp. 608–615.

on this theme. Sri Aurobindo, connecting onto the Hindu tradition and expanding on it, refers to three avatars: Christ, Krishna, and Buddha. Yet in the analysis, both Christ and Buddha are said not to belong to the category of avatar. The statement in question, made by the author of the book *Meditations on the Tarot,* is: "As well as Buddha, therefore, it is necessary to eliminate Jesus Christ, also, from the abridged list of avatars given by Sri Aurobindo. Thus, only Krishna remains, who is, in addition to Rama, the avatar par excellence of Hinduism." However, in *Meditations on the Tarot* we also find the following striking statement: "The Kalki Avatar awaited by the Hindus and the Maitreya Buddha awaited by the Buddhists will manifest in a single personality." In light of this statement, a single personality will manifest both as a buddha (*awakened one:* ascent of the human) and as an avatar (*revelatory one:* descent of the divine). This statement relating to Maitreya–Kalki can also be applied to Jesus Christ and Gautama Buddha—that is, Jesus/Gautama (awakened ones: ascent of the human) and Christ/Buddha (*revelatory ones:* descent of the divine).

A closer reading of this analysis reveals that the author of *Meditations on the Tarot* is applying the definition of buddhas and avatars in a certain way *to illustrate the difference in principle between a buddha and an avatar.* In the case of Gautama Buddha, the author brings out the human side of Gautama, which reveals the highest level of pure humanism. In the case of Jesus Christ, he indicates that Christ is far more than an Avatar "for the liberation of the good and the destruction of the wicked" (*Bhagavad Gita* iv, 8).

A fair conclusion would be that all of the listed names: Krishna, Buddha, Christ, and Maitreya–Kalki can be viewed in either way—as *Buddha* or as *Avatar* according to whether one adopts a Buddhist or a Hindu perspective. However, in the case of Jesus Christ, it is a matter of a being who simultaneously manifests the highest aspect of a Buddha and as an Avatar, yet is beyond the categories of buddha and avatar. And in the case of Gautama Buddha, Buddhists tend to emphasize the purely human qualities, and Hindus (not all, but many) tend to see Gautama Buddha as an Avatar—this being the perspective of Sri Aurobindo. As long as all of this is borne in mind, the seeming contradiction referred to at the start of this note, while being a contradiction on the level of definitions, is ultimately not a contradiction in essence.

APPENDIX 3

THE FOUNDATION STONE MEDITATION

This important meditation is referred to in appendix 2, section (4), in connection with the impulse of the Maitreya, which, according to Valentin Tomberg, comes to expression particularly in the fourth verse. The text of the Foundation Stone meditation follows these introductory words—see below. It was given by Rudolf Steiner on Christmas Day 1923 as a meditation enfolding a suprasensory reality called by various names: the Holy Grail and the Philosophers' Stone being two of the more traditional designations for what Rudolf Steiner called the *Foundation Stone of Love*. He indicated that through living deeply and intensively with this meditation one is able to receive the *Foundation Stone of Love* into one's heart.

This meditation was given at a special moment in time, at the onset of the Second Coming of Christ. The first three verses of the Foundation Stone meditation are *addressed to the human soul by Christ* at this time of his return in a suprasensory form in the world of life forces, the ethereal realm. It is in an ethereal form and as a moral force in Nature—*"in the clouds," "like lightning flashing from the east and shining in the west"*—that he is manifesting himself now at this time of his Second Coming.

The Foundation Stone meditation is a powerful source of attunement to this new manifestation of Christ. It encapsulates the event corresponding in our time to the Baptism in the River Jordan two thousand years ago. At that time John the Baptist spoke the words, *"Behold the Lamb of God"*—indicating Christ (the Lamb) incarnating into the human being of Jesus of Nazareth as a Presence on the physical level of our planet Earth. Now, in our time, the laying of the *Foundation Stone of Love* through Rudolf Steiner is an expression of the baptismal event of Christ's Second Coming, heralding his Presence in the ethereal realm enveloping and permeating Mother Earth. Through the *Foundation Stone of Love* one is "baptized" into the Second Coming of Christ. Rudolf Steiner, as the human being through whom this meditation was given to humanity, had the role of a modern-day "John the Baptist," as the one whose task was to herald the coming of Christ in the ethereal realm.

The first three verses of the Foundation Stone meditation—addressed to the human soul by Christ—each begin with the words *human soul.* The fourth verse is an answer—or echo—from the human being, as a prayer to Christ in his suprasensory form, in response to the first three verses.

The special connection of the fourth verse to the theme of this book is referred to above. The fourth verse refers to the Mystery of Golgotha as evolution's turning point of time through the birth of the true "I"—bestowed upon humanity through the coming of Christ two thousand years ago. The fourth verse culminates in a prayer offered to Christ in his suprasensory form, a prayer that is highly appropriate for our time.

The structure and content of the Foundation Stone meditation reveal the essence of Christ's gift to humanity at this time of the Second Coming—bestowing an impulse elevating the human soul to an awareness of a living relationship with the Eternal Trinity and with the nine levels of celestial hierarchies weaving in the whole of creation in service of the Godhead (see next page).

Working with the Foundation Stone meditation can be a powerful individual practice. Each of the four verses of the meditation leads to a deep and profound experience of the *Foundation Stone of Love.* In this sense it is a fulfillment of the *hidden knowledge*

Angels (Guardian Spirits of individuals)	Moon sphere
Archangels (Guardian Spirits of peoples)	Mercury sphere
Archai (Guardian Spirits of epochs of time)	Venus sphere
Exusiai (Elohim, Powers, Spirits of Form)	Sun sphere
Dynamis (Mights, Virtues, Spirits of Movement)	Sun sphere
Kyriotetes (Dominions, Lords, Spirits of Wisdom)	Sun sphere
Thrones (Spirits of Will, Beings of the Word)	Mars sphere
Cherubim (Spirits of Wisdom and Harmony)	Jupiter sphere
Seraphim (Spirits of Love, Beings of Memory)	Saturn sphere

of the Grail, spoken of by Rudolf Steiner in his book *An Outline of Esoteric Science:*

> The Christ Mystery will increasingly permeate our life of ideas, feeling, and will. "Hidden" Grail knowledge will become evident; as an inner force, it will increasingly permeate the manifestations of human life. (p. 389)

THE FOUNDATION STONE MEDITATION

Human Soul!
Thou livest in the limbs
Which bear thee through the World of Space
Into the Spirit's Ocean Being.
Practice Spirit Recollection
In depths of soul,
Where in the Wielding Will
 of World Creating
Thine own "I"
Comes to being in God's "I."
And thou wilt truly live
In Human World Being.
For the Father Spirit
 of the Heights holds sway
In Depths of Worlds
Begetting Being:
Seraphim, Cherubim, Thrones!
Let there ring out from the Heights
What in the Depths is echoed.
This speaks:
Ex Deo nascimur.[1]
The Spirits of the Elements hear it:
In East, West, North, South—
May human beings hear it.

---

1   The literal meaning of the Latin Rosicrucian mantra *"Ex Deo nascimur"*
  is "From God we are born." An alternate translation from the Latin, as
  indicated by Rudolf Steiner, is "From the Divine, humanity is born."

Human Soul!
Thou livest in the beat of heart and lung
Which leads thee through the Rhythm of Time
Into the realm of thine own soul's feeling.
Practice Spirit Awareness
In balance of the soul,
Where the Surging Deeds
 of the World's Becoming
Thine own "I"
Unite with the World "I."
And thou wilt truly feel
In Human Soul Weaving.
For the Christ Will
 in the encircling Round holds sway
In Rhythms of Worlds
Bestowing Grace on the soul:
Kyriotetes, Dynamis, Exusiai!
Let there be fired from the East
What in the West is formed.
This speaks:
In Christo morimur.[2]
The Spirits of the Elements hear it:
In East, West, North, South—
May human beings hear it.

---

2   The literal meaning of this Latin Rosicrucian mantra is "In Christ we
     die." An alternate translation from the Latin, as indicated by Rudolf
     Steiner, is "In Christ, death becomes life."

Human Soul!
Thou livest in the resting head
Which from the Grounds of Eternity
Opens to thee the World Thoughts.
Practice Spirit Beholding
In stillness of thought,
Where the Eternal Aims of Gods
World Being's Light
On thine own "I" bestow
For thy free willing.
And thou wilt truly think
In Human Spirit Foundations.
For the World Thoughts
 of the Spirit hold sway
In Beings of Worlds
Beseeching Light:
Archai, Archangeloi, Angeloi!
Let there be prayed from the Depths
What in the Heights will be granted.
This speaks:
Per Spiritum Sanctum reviviscimus.[3]
The Spirits of the Elements hear it:
In East, West, North, South—
May human beings hear it.

---

3   The literal translation from the Latin of this Rosicrucian mantra is
     "Through the Holy Spirit the soul is revived." An alternate translation
     from Latin, as indicated by Rudolf Steiner, is "Through the world-
     thoughts of the Spirit, the soul awakens."

At the turning point of time
The Spirit Light of the World
Entered the Stream of Earthly Being.
Darkness of Night had held its sway.
Day-radiant Light streamed into human souls:
Light that gives warmth
To simple Shepherds' Hearts.
Light that enlightens
The wise Heads of Kings.
O Light Divine,
O Christ Sun,
Warm Thou our hearts,
Enlighten Thou our heads,
That Good may become—
What from our hearts we found
And from our heads direct
With single purpose.

Bibliography

Andreev, Daniel. *The Rose of the World*. Hudson, NY: Lindisfarne Books, 1997.

Anonymous. *Meditations on the Tarot: A Journey into Christian Hermeticism*. New York: Tarcher-Putnam, 2002.

Emmerich, Anne Catherine. *Visions of the Life of Christ*. Taos, NM: LogoSophia, 2014.

Isaacson, Estelle. *Through the Eyes of Mary Magdalene*, 2 vols. Taos, NM: LogoSophia, 2012.

Kirchner-Bockholt, Erich and Margarete. *Rudolf Steiner's Mission and Ita Wegman*. London: Rudolf Steiner Press, 1997 (private publication).

Meyer, T. H., and Elizabeth Vreede. *The Bodhisattva Question: Krishnamurti, Rudolf Steiner, Valentin Tomberg, and the Mystery of the Twentieth-Century Master*. London: Temple Lodge, 1993.

O'Leary, Paul V., ed. *The Inner Life of the Earth: Exploring the Mysteries of Nature, Subnature, and Supranature*. Great Barrington, MA: SteinerBooks, 2008.

Oldenberg, Hermann. *Buddha: His Life, His Doctrine, His Order*. London-Edinburgh: Williams and Norgate, 1882.

Powell, Robert. *The Christ Mystery: Reflections on the Second Coming*. Fair Oaks, CA: Rudolf Steiner College Press, 1999.

———. *Chronicle of the Living Christ: The Life and Ministry of Jesus Christ : Foundations of Cosmic Christianity*. Hudson, NY: Anthroposophic Press, 1996.

———. *Cultivating Inner Radiance and the Body of Immortality*. Great Barrington, MA: SteinerBooks, 2012.

———. *Hermetic Astrology, vol. 1.: Astrology and Reincarnation*. San Rafael, CA: Sophia Foundation Press, 2007.

———, ed. *Journal for Star Wisdom*. Great Barrington, MA: SteinerBooks/Lindisfarne Books, annual publication.

———. *Prophecy–Phenomena–Hope: The Real Meaning of the year 2012*. Great Barrington, Massachusetts: SteinerBooks, 2011.

Powell, Robert, and David Bowden. *Astrogeographia: Correspondences between the Stars and Earthly Locations*. Great Barrington, MA: SteinerBooks, 2012.

Powell, Robert, and Kevin Dann. *Christ and the Maya Calendar: 2012 and the Coming of the Antichrist*. Great Barrington, MA: Steiner-Books, 2009.

Rau, Christoph. *Die beiden Jesusknaben und die Messiaserwartung der Essener*. Stuttgart: Verlag Johannes Mayer, 2010.

Scahill, Jeremy. *Dirty Wars: The World is a Battlefield*. New York: Nation Books, 2013.

Solovyov, Vladimir. *War, Progress, and the End of History: Three Conversations, Including a Short Tale of the Antichrist*. Hudson, NY: Lindisfarne Press, 1990.

Steiner, Rudolf. *According to Luke: The Gospel of Compassion and Love Revealed*. Great Barrington, MA: SteinerBooks, 2001.

———. *According to Matthew: The Gospel of Christ's Humanity*. Great Barrington, MA: Anthroposophic Press, 2003.

———. *Background to the Gospel of St. Mark*. London: Rudolf Steiner Press, 1968.

———. *The Book of Revelation and the Work of the Priest*. London: Rudolf Steiner Press, 1998.

———. *Deeper Secrets of Human History in the Light of the Gospel of St. Matthew*. London: Rudolf Steiner Press, 1985.

———. *Esoteric Christianity and the Mission of Christian Rosenkreutz*. London: Rudolf Steiner Press, 2001.

———. *Esoteric Lessons 1910–1912: From the Esoteric School*, vol. 2. Great Barrington, MA: SteinerBooks, 2013.

———. *The Festivals and Their Meaning*. London: Rudolf Steiner Press, 1996.

———. *Four Mystery Plays*. London: Anthroposophical Publishing Company, 1925.

———. *"Freemasonry" and Ritual Work: The Misraim Service*. Great Barrington, MA: SteinerBooks, 2007.

———. *From the History and Contents of the First Section of the Esoteric School, 1904–1914*. Great Barrington, MA: SteinerBooks, 2010.

———. *From Jesus to Christ*. London: Rudolf Steiner Press, 1973.

———. *The Gospel of St. John*. Hudson, NY: Anthroposophic Press, 1984.

———. *The Incarnation of Ahriman: The Embodiment of Evil*. London: Rudolf Steiner Press, 2006.

———. *The Gospel of St. Matthew*. London: Rudolf Steiner Press, 1965.

———. *The Reappearance of Christ in the Etheric*. Great Barrington, MA: SteinerBooks, 2003.

———. *The Spiritual Hierarchies and the Physical World: Zodiac, Planets, and Cosmos*. Great Barrington, MA: SteinerBooks, 1996.

————. *The True Nature of the Second Coming*. London: Rudolf Steiner Press, 1971.

————. *Über die astrale Welt und das Devachan*. Dornach, Switzerland: Rudolf Steiner Verlag, 1996.

————. *Wonders of the World, Ordeals of the Soul, Revelations of the Spirit*. London: Rudolf Steiner Press, 1963.

Tomberg, Valentin. *Christ and Sophia: Anthroposophic Meditations on the Old Testament, New Testament, and Apocalypse*. Great Barrington, MA: SteinerBooks, 2006.

von Halle, Judith. *Descent into the Depths of the Earth on the Anthroposophic Path of Schooling*. London: Temple Lodge, 2011.

ABOUT THE AUTHORS

ROBERT POWELL has an enduring passion for the stars, and was awarded a PhD for his contribution to the History of the Zodiac. He is an internationally renowned lecturer. Through the content of his talks at conferences and workshops, his living knowledge of the stars is woven into his presentations. As well as being a scholar of the history of astronomy, Robert is also a movement therapist trained in the art of eurythmy (from the Greek meaning beautiful, harmonious movement). Focusing upon the cosmic aspects of eurythmy he founded the Choreocosmos School of Cosmic and Sacred Dance, and he leads cosmic dances (dancing with the stars) in endeavoring to create harmony between the heavens, the Earth, humanity, and nature. He presents Choreocosmos workshops in various parts of the world, including Australia, Europe, and North America. Robert is also cofounder of the Sophia Foundation and the Sophia Grail Circle, through which he facilitates sacred celebrations dedicated to the Divine Feminine. With Karen Rivers, cofounder of the Sophia Foundation, he leads pilgrimages to the world's sacred sites: Turkey, 1996; the Holy Land, 1997; France, 1998; Britain, 2000; Italy, 2002; Greece, 2004; Egypt, 2006; India, 2008; Turkey, 2009; the Grand Canyon, 2010; South Africa, 2012; and Peru, 2014.

Robert is the author of many books, including *The Astrological Revolution* and *Christ and the Maya Calendar* (both coauthored by Kevin Dann); *The Mystery, Biography & Destiny of Mary Magdalene* and *Prophecy–Phenomena–Hope: The Real Meaning of 2012.* Robert is also editor of the yearly *Journal for Star Wisdom.* He also wrote two books with Lacquanna Paul: *Cosmic Dances of the Zodiac* and *Cosmic Dances of the Planets,* which not only describe cosmic dance but also contain a wealth of research material. For texts relating to sacred dance, see *The Prayer Sequence in Sacred Dance* and *The Foundation Stone Meditation in the Sacred Dance of Eurythmy* (both written with Lacquanna Paul). Robert's most recent books are *Cultivating Inner Radiance and the Body of Immortality,* outlining a path through eurythmy to Christ, and *Astrogeographia: Correspondences between the Stars and Earthly Locations* (coauthored by David Bowden). For further information on his books and courses, visit:

www.sophiafoundation.org or www.astrogeographia.org
or steinerbooks.org/books/AuthorDetail.aspx?id=23981

ESTELLE ISAACSON is a contemporary mystic and seer whose first two books were published by LogoSophia in 2012: *Through the Eyes of Mary Magdalene: Early Years and Soul Awakening.* In this first book in a trilogy on the life of Mary Magdalene, Estelle Isaacson presents her visions of the life of "the Apostle to the Apostles" as seen through Magdalene's own eyes. The second book, *Through the Eyes of Mary Magdalene: From Initiation to the Passion,* enters the profound mysteries of Christ's Passion, culminating in the Resurrection.

www.ingramcontent.com/pod-product-compliance
Lightning Source LLC
Chambersburg PA
CBHW020201090426
42734CB00008B/903